Beyond the Walls

*The Story of One Man's Journey from
Prison to Freedom... and Back Again*

CARL CARLSON
FOUNDER/DIRECTOR, MEN OF VALOR

WESTBOW
PRESS
A DIVISION OF THOMAS NELSON
& ZONDERVAN

WestBow Press books may be ordered through booksellers or by contacting:

WestBow Press
A Division of Thomas Nelson & Zondervan
1663 Liberty Drive
Bloomington, IN 47403
www.westbowpress.com
1 (866) 928-1240

ISBN: 978-1-4908-3351-4 (sc)
ISBN: 978-1-4908-3352-1 (e)

Library of Congress Control Number: 2014906370

Print information available on the last page.

WestBow Press rev. date: 5/20/2015

Contents

Foreword

Forget the former things; do not dwell in the past. See, I am doing a new thing! Now it springs up; do you not perceive it? I am making a way in the wilderness and streams in the wasteland. ~ Isaiah 43:18-19

It was 1980 when I first met Carl Carlson. I was the 29-year old Director of Urban Services for the Nashville YMCA. The Nashville Y had a long history of helping troubled youth, and at the time had joined forces with the Nashville Juvenile Detention Center. I was in the process of finding someone to run our recreation program. My boss, Jim Rayhab, had been in conversation with officials at the detention center who told him about a student intern named Carl Carlson. On crutches after a recent knee surgery, I hobbled over to meet this man. I was caught completely off guard by the heavily bearded, 6'2" 33-year old Vietnam veteran who looked more like a mountain man than a coach. Little did I know the plans God was putting in place that would change our lives and impact thousands over the next 34 years....

Carl has an intensity about him that is unmatched. Although I can't recall the exact conversation we had that day, I instinctively knew that hiring this man would be an enormous asset for the kids in the detention center. Believing in the importance of a strong relationship with God and the guidance of the Holy Spirit, I was impressed that Carl was thankful to God for delivering him from a life of crime and incarceration. Over time I would learn the incredible story of this man who had experienced pain, neglect, abandonment, and violence as a child. As a young adult he had been a seemingly incorrigible felon—until his destiny was changed forever by an encounter with Jesus Christ while in prison. That unique intensity was about to be channeled in a way the prophet Isaiah would recognize. God was working in Carl to overcome his past and do things for the Kingdom.

Although I didn't know any of it at the time, God had already been doing amazing things in preparing Carl for this very place. I still don't know how Carl amassed enough college credit to be close to graduating from Trevecca Nazarene College (now a university) when he had only been out of jail for a short time. Then I met his girlfriend, Karen, who was soon to become his wife. It seemed as if God had sent down one of his top angels to keep Carl on track. Carl's gift for working with troubled kids was obvious. I recall one particular counseling session where a tough street kid just broke down and shared his pain with Carl after only a few minutes. It wasn't so much what was said that impacted me, as the eye contact between them and Carl's innate ability to connect and gain trust. He is authentic in a way that can pierce your soul. Breaking through the emotional barriers that people build up is one of the most difficult things to accomplish in counseling. Carl is a natural at relationship building and helping people move forward with their lives.

When Carl speaks, people listen. It didn't take long for he and the detention center chaplain—Ed Hunley—to begin bringing people together in a shared vision. The two were about to intervene in the lives of youngsters brought into the juvenile justice system in a way that would impact them for good. The number of volunteers grew as folks were compelled to get involved. During the mid-1980's I was able to secure a grant from the Tennessee Commission on Children and Youth for an endeavor called Y-CAP (the YMCA Community Action Project). The concept behind Y-CAP was to work with juvenile first offenders in an effort to keep them from committing a second offense. Since approximately

80% of crime in America is committed by repeat offenders, Y-CAP, if successful, would be part of the solution in reducing crime in our community. With funding from the state, the obvious person to lead the charge was Carl Carlson.

There are numerous stories I could relate about the twelve years that followed, but that would take another book. Suffice it to say that under Carl's leadership, Y-CAP became recognized by the Juvenile Court Judges of America as one of the top ten juvenile prevention/intervention programs in the United States. Y-CAP's budget grew from around $50,000 to in excess of $1,000,000 and eventually became its own YMCA center with a renovated building and gymnasium in the heart of inner-city Nashville. With the help of a hard working staff and countless volunteers, God was blessing this community, and the prophet Isaiah's words were becoming reality, as a way was being made in the wilderness and streams had begun flowing in the wasteland.

Working with Carl was challenging. He and I were then, and still are, often on opposite ends of the spectrum when it comes to certain subjects. In sports, for example, he is a diehard Dallas Cowboy fan, and I grew up in Pittsburgh ("Sixburgh") Steeler country. As for politics, I tend to be liberal, where he is conservative. He often reminds me that it's a good thing we didn't meet when I was a student protesting the Vietnam war and he was a returning vet. But the love of Jesus, love for family, and a unified commitment to the same goal promotes acceptance over differences, and Carl and I are bonded as brothers in Christ.

In 1995 when Carl left Y-CAP and the YMCA, our work relationship naturally changed. I much preferred being a supporter of what God was calling him to do, anyway. Being his friend was far simpler than being his supervisor. It isn't easy supervising a maverick! After Y-CAP, Carl spent a year "in the wilderness," seeking God. It eventually became clear that it was time to start a new ministry. This time he would be working with men behind bars. He was about to come full circle from where he had started—going back now into the prisons from which he had expected—and hoped—never to return.

As you read *Beyond the Walls*, you will learn of the amazing work of the Men of Valor prison ministry—a dynamic intervention and aftercare program for incarcerated men and their families. The nascent stages were filled with prayer and a gathering of men Carl had asked the Lord to bring together for wisdom and resources. Once again, as with Y-CAP, Carl threw himself into the task of recruiting volunteers and mentors to bring about what could only be called "a new thing." The prophet Isaiah would recognize this man as a brother. The things that are happening behind prison walls through Men of Valor's "Jericho Project," as well as in their holistic aftercare component, are helping transform desperate lives into lives filled with hope and success. Families are being restored, hope is being realized, and recidivism is being significantly reduced. This is an exemplary model that should be replicated throughout the United States.

With nearly all men in prison, the one common thing missing is hope. Without hope it's impossible to have a vision. And without vision, as Jeremiah reminds us, the people will perish. Carl found out many years ago, however, that when you have a relationship with God, you find hope. People who have known Carl through the years are familiar with the phrase, "We're in a war out there." This, of course, refers to the serious consequences of the social conditions which lead to poverty, crime, and loss of dignity.

If something is worth doing, get serious about it and give it your all. No excuses. This has always been Carl's full determination, and it has guided him well. His faith in God has provided him a clear path for making the right choices in life. Because of this philosophy, he continues to inspire others who are not afraid of the hard work it takes to achieve seemingly impossible goals.

Beyond the Walls is a book about one man's ability to overcome hardship and despair and rise to new heights through the love, mercy and grace of Jesus Christ. With this has come untold blessings. Carl considers his family to be his greatest blessing, after salvation. He and Karen have raised four sons: Joshua, Philip, Michael and Stephen. Josh has a wonderful position at Vanderbilt University Medical Center in Nashville. His beautiful wife, Janna, works for Men of Valor as Carl's executive administrative assistant. Through the years Philip has worked alongside Carl in ministering to the children of men in prison. Currently Philip is in the heating and air conditioning business and is doing very well. Michael and Stephen have both followed their father's footsteps in the military and are currently serving our country as United States Marines.

Although Carl's story is unique, he would be the first to point out that for anyone who seeks the Lord, "all things are possible through Christ who strengthens us." It is this amazing hope and promise that Carl shared first with juvenile offenders, then with hardened prisoners, and ultimately with all those who have joined him in the effort to bring the light of God's love to the world. If anyone ever doubts there is a good God who cares about people and justice, they can look to the life of Carl Carlson for assurance. His is a story of redemption, grace, and accomplishment. It is a story that gives us all hope.

J. Lawrence
Nashville, Tennessee
August 2014

Acknowledgements

The greatest blessing God has given me, next to my wife and sons, is the number of men and women he has brought into my life. These are people who have believed in me and supported me in this ministry to men who are incarcerated and their families. I could name hundreds and will regret leaving some off this list, but here is a sampling of the incredible men and women who have supported me, and in some cases mentored me, over these many years:

First of all, Karen's family: her late father Vernon Brown, her mother and stepfather Terry and Frances Acker, her brother Michael (Micky) Brown, and her brother and sister-in-law Jeff and Stephanie Brown; also Adam Hicks, Overton and Robin Thompson, Jack and Elizabeth Wallace, Larry and Karen Kloess, Dr. David and Vicki Watts, the late Dr. Millard Reed (my former pastor), Steve Reed, Pastor Doug Runyon, Pastor Kevin Ulmet (my current pastor), Pastor Dan Boone (current president of Trevecca Nazarene University), Dr. Norman Henry, Dr. Tom Duncan, Judge and

Claire Drowota, Pastor Bruce Oldham, Pastor Brent Lawrence, Pastor Jack Galloway, Pastor Jim Bachmann, Pastor Carter Crenshaw, Pastor Lee Woolery, Pastor Gary Henecke, Sam Anderson, Sonny and Laurie Lyons, Andy Wilson, John and Martha Oman, Teryna Edwards, Joanne Pulles, Thomas Purifoy, David Black, Frank Burkholder, John and Sarah Avery, William Taylor, John and Sara Chilton, Ken and Ava Laws, Everett Holmes, Bill Calkin, Meredith Flautt, Eddie Hutton, Steve Merryman, Tom Ozburn, Bill Clark, Don and Kat Zimmerman, John and Carole Ferguson, Damon and Carrie Hininger, Steve Groom, Jerry Jennings, Tom Smith, Larry Baker, Randy Haviland, Henry McFadden, Bill Turner, Tony Giarratana, Gregg Turner, Jim and Berenice Denton, Jerry Breast, Ty Osman, Kirby Davis, Bill Freeman, Cal Turner, Cabot Pyle, Runcie Clements, Jack Hooper, David Hooven, Paul and Susan Rutledge, Russ Harms, Louis Joseph, Wearen Hughes, Chuck Seaman, Joel Perry, Cammy Bethea, Mike and Pam Shampain, Steve Butler, Myra Ishee, Sheriff Daron Hall, Don Knotts, Ben Sensing, Wilbur Sensing, Jameson Norton, Bill Brown, Darwin Holt, Daryl Murray, David Bradley, Tate Lamastus, David Caldwell, Brad Warren, Brett Warren, Bruce Francis, Chuck Elcan, Sam Jones, John Sawyer, Kevin Gangaware, Lee Beaman, Margaret Burke, Matt Dunlap, Jim Gardner, Jimmy Spradley, James Stansell, Jake Stansell, David Stansell, David Post Sr., David

Post Jr., Gary Herndon, Gordon Steele, Charles Irby, Brett Beavers, Charlie Finchum, Mike Servais, Jack Blier, Tom Firestone, John Sugg, Billy Goad, Jimmy Spruill, Howard Spruill, David King, Toby Williams, Steve Childress, Trent Hemphill, Larry McCormack, Jay Hoover, Shane Finch, Mike Check, David Pitzer, Steve and Minna Rasmussen, Rick and Andrea Carlton, David Waynick, Roland Smith, Thad and Darlene Guerra, Dr. Paul Stumb, Bill Hoffman, David Rice, Rusty Dixon, Richard Anderson, Frederick Oechsner, Jeb Beasley, Scott Perry, Mark Farr, Brian Reyes, Karla McDonald, Sam McDonald, Billy Rowland, Walter Spires, Don Bruce, Chris Bishop, Norris Nielson, Mark Weller, Matt Cowan, Wayne Bratcher, Jude Lenahan (my former prosecutor), Doug Brandon, the late Gerald Skinner, Tom Pate, Jim Pate, Ray Dey, Jim Beavers, Russell Brothers, Steve Thorne, Clark Baker, and most of all, Jimmy Webb, Phil Hickey, Bill Lee, John Grayken, Louie Buntin, J.D. Elliott, Ed Hunley, Jim Denton, Chet Leone, Ken Leary, and J. Lawrence. A special thank you to Jeff and Amy Dobyns for underwriting the cost of having this book published.

Last, there is the Men of Valor staff—the greatest people anyone could ever hope to work with: Curt Campbell, Raul Lopez, Tevin Peterson, Marcus Martin, Chad Daniels, Frank Turner, Tommy Mathis, Chet Leone, Ken Leary, Dale Still, JR Davis, Jennifer Wenberg, Donna Mayo, Marlo Wilt, Anthony Charles,

Andy Dodson, John Michalak, Darnell Ford, and my beloved daughter-in-law, Janna Carlson. These people are in the "trenches" every day fighting the fight, doing all they can to bring HOPE to many, many folks. They are simply the best!

Dedication

This book is dedicated to my wife, Karen, who has been my encourager and sounding board for 34 years. It is dedicated to our four sons—Joshua, Philip, Michael, and Stephen—who have been my strength and joy, and to our daughter in law, Janna, who has joined not only our family but also this ministry with all her heart and soul. Lastly, it is to my younger brother Phillip, who was the first person to ever tell me the story of Jesus. To the countless men and women who have supported and prayed over the ministries God has entrusted me with, I am forever in your debt. Nothing I have done for the Kingdom has been accomplished on my own.

Sons are a heritage from the Lord, children a reward from him. Like arrows in the cloths of a warrior are sons born in one's youth. Blessed is the man whose quiver is full of them. (Psalm 127: 3-5, NIV)

I can do all things through Christ Jesus who strengthens me. (Philippians 4:13)

Author's Note

A number of men over the years tried to convince me to write a book, but to no avail. First of all, I just didn't have the time, and secondly, I wondered who on earth would want to read my story. When Jeff Dobyns contacted a publisher, laid out the money, and invited Lyn Cryderman to fly from New York to Nashville to interview me, I finally agreed to do it. Since the Lord touched me in a prison cell in 1979, my journey changed from a fight for survival to an adventure in Christ. To this day, I struggle with "demons" from my past, but God's grace has been sufficient. Whatever good I have tried to do with my life, **He receives all the credit and glory**. The Lord, my wife Karen, and my four sons have been my strength.

Everything in this book is true, but it may not all be accurate. The combination of a hazy memory and perhaps wanting to forget some of my past may have clouded some of the details of my earlier years. Some names have been changed for various reasons. I am not wanting to hurt the descendants of people who may have been involved in my upbringing or my crimes. The old saying goes, "the devil is in the details," and that always seemed to be the case with me. Looking back, however, I know that it was God who was in the details. For only He could have worked all this together for the good. What is absolutely certain is that I would not be here today without the redemptive love and transforming grace of Jesus Christ.

1

I've Never Seen So
Many Diamonds

It was a sitting duck; a treasure chest just waiting for us to dip our hands into the gold and diamonds like the pirates of yesteryear. We had cased the joint earlier and could hardly believe our good fortune. For a smaller store, it had a huge inventory—I'd never seen so many diamonds! An old guy—probably the owner—closed the joint by himself every night at 8:00. By 8:15 he was gone, and at 9:00 the other stores in the strip mall shut down. The place was like a ghost town by 10:00.

The four of us had met the day before. I was working as the head bouncer at the largest nightclub in southern New Jersey, with about sixteen bouncers reporting to me, including, ironically, four off-duty cops. The money was good, but I never seemed to be able to hold onto it very long, so I was always looking to moonlight and I wasn't too choosy about the jobs I took. One day

I got a call from a guy I knew whose friend wanted his business burned down. I'd never done anything like that, but how hard could it be to light a match to something? Turns out, harder than I thought. I filled up a five-gallon can with gasoline and met my friend at the soon-to-become insurance claim—a hardware store. He had the keys to the joint, so we just walked in and I began splashing gasoline all over the place. I started at the back of the store and backed up toward the front door, emptying the can as I went. When we got to the door, I lit a match and BOOM! The blast knocked us off our feet and onto our backs, singeing our hair and nearly blinding us. We were lucky to get out of that one alive, but it was a quick $10,000 for me, even if it temporarily cost me my eyebrows.

Only the stupid get caught

I never gave things like that much thought; never considered the danger it caused for the firefighters who responded; never cared that I was breaking the law. Easy money—that's all it was to me. I also never worried much about getting caught—that's what happened to the stupid ones. I was too smart to get caught.

One night as I got back to my apartment after closing down the club, one of my buddies called to tell me that he and two other guys were heading to Nashville and needed someone with my "experience." I had taken out a jewelry store on my own, and word had gotten around that I knew the ropes when it came to this kind of job. The timing couldn't have been better. My last job was a pretty brazen heist I committed in broad daylight with another friend at a jewelry store in Florida. We walked in, waving our guns in the air just like in the movies, ordering everybody onto the floor as we helped ourselves to diamond necklaces and bracelets, gold rings, Rolex watches, you name it. We netted around $10,000, even though the stuff was worth a lot more. Just the cost of doing business. When you try to fence a suitcase full of jewelry, there's not much room for negotiation. You drive to an abandoned lot, meet a couple of guys driving a black Lincoln, open your trunk and show 'em the "product," take whatever they offer, then hope you make it to your car without getting a bullet in the back of your head.

I blew through that ten grand in about two weeks on bad investments, girls, booze, dope, and gambling. My usual hobbies. I wasn't much for saving for a rainy day. The way I looked at things, if it rained, I could always find a way to get my hands on more money. So when my buddy called, I was all ears because I needed some quick cash to replenish my entertainment account. From what he told me, this would provide that and more. Even after splitting the take among the four of us, we'd walk away with about $50,000 each. Pretty good money in the early 1970's.

We drove down to Nashville and checked into a motel on the south side of the city a couple miles from the store we planned to rob. On the trip down I'd gotten to know the two new guys pretty well, but I was always leery of getting into "business opportunities" with guys I didn't know. In most other businesses, if you make a mistake you get chewed out by your boss. In my business, someone screws up and you end up in jail. Or worse. These guys seemed pretty cool, plus I knew my buddy wouldn't recruit a couple of rookies for a job like this. But when one of them suggested we all pay a visit to the store the next day posing as customers to give the joint one last look, I got nervous.

"That's the stupidest thing I've ever heard," I said. "Four men walking into a jewelry store in the middle of the day asking to look at rings? Are you crazy?"

I was about to walk out and take the next bus back to New Jersey when my buddy calmed me down and assured me these two guys were solid. I had my doubts, but we decided I would head over to the store, look it over, and based on what I learned, figure out the best way to get the goods and get out of there.

The plan we came up with was as simple as the job itself. We would drive in two cars to the store, go inside, put everybody on the floor, rob it, and get out as quickly as possible. Even if we could not hear the security alarm go off, we had to assume it would and would go directly to the local police station.

It went off pretty smoothly. We grabbed as much as we could, nobody got hurt, and when my instincts told me the cops were on their way, I gave the signal.

"Everybody out!" I hissed, and just like that, it was over.

Well, almost. We still had to get back to the motel without attracting any attention. Four guys dressed in black walking down the sidewalk carrying duffel bags wasn't exactly an Einstein move, so we each took a different route back to the motel. As I doubled back and forth on a circuitous route, it crossed my mind that the rest of the team could easily have recruited me for my expertise, all the while planning to jump me back at the motel, take my bag, and drop me off a bridge on their way out of town. It happens. Fortunately I got back before the others and kept my guard up as they returned, but my fears were unfounded. It was all backslapping and laughter as we dumped our take out on one of the rickety double beds. We hit that store pretty good—I'd never seen so many diamonds in my life! I had already informed my fence that I would be stopping by with some quality stuff for him to sell, and I couldn't wait to get back and dump it in exchange for a nice wad of cash. I have to admit, I was pretty proud of the way we pulled it off. I lit a cigarette and cracked open a beer to celebrate as we split the loot.

"Hey, I'm one of you!"

Once everyone had their fair share, we headed out the door to drive back to New Jersey when I saw them: more cops than I'd ever seen before in one place. I mean, man, they had the place surrounded! I had no idea who ratted us out, but at that instant I didn't really care. I'd deal with that later. All I knew was that I wasn't going to jail. As luck would have it, a guy had just gotten out of his car, which was parked outside our room. So I did what any respectable armed robber would do when the police are moving in. I put a gun to the guy's head in plain view of the police and yelled at them to back off. With a hostage, we'd at least have a chance.

I motioned for the hostage to get back behind the wheel of his Cadillac. I had no idea what the other guys were doing; in this kind of work, it was every man for himself.

"Take off," I snarled, with the gun still pointed at his head. "Whatever you do, just don't let 'em catch us!"

Even serious crime has its lighter moments. As my hostage hit the accelerator and peeled past the cop cars, he pleaded, "Hey, I'm one of you guys." Turns out he had a trunk full of drugs and was in Nashville to make a little money himself. I couldn't believe my good fortune because our hostage had every reason to outrun the police lest he land in the clinker himself. And once we got away, I might even score some free drugs from him.

But my streak of luck was short lived, another chronic issue in my line of work. The cops must have decided to risk losing a hostage in order to bring us to justice because our rear-view mirror was filled with red and blue flashing lights. The chase was on, with all those cops now speeding after us as we tried our best to lose them. The only problem was that I didn't know my way around Nashville, and with every turn we just kept getting more confused. We finally got on a road that seemed like a highway, and my new partner really opened her up. That old Cadillac was putting some distance between the cops and us, and it looked like we just might make it. But we soon learned what happens when a 1968 Cadillac takes a hairpin turn at ninety. Fortunately all we hit was a couple of mailboxes and a road sign, but the car was wedged tightly in a ditch, and it was clear we weren't going anywhere unless we crawled out and took off on foot. Which was exactly what we were in the process of doing when the parade of policemen arrived, this time with guns drawn and not in a very good mood. I weighed my options and demonstrated the first good sense I'd had in the past twenty-four hours.

I surrendered.

In the confusion one of our guys—Nathan—got away; just ran off as the chase was happening, and as far as I know, he never got caught. One of the other guys—Jack—was caught, made bond and within a year was shot to death in New Jersey. He never did a day of time for this crime, but he paid for it in another way. Tony, the last guy, was also caught and was on his way to jail with me.

They set our bond so high I didn't have the money to pay it. All I had on hand was the jewelry, and it's not like they were going to let me fence it to pay my bond. I learned later the reason they set our bond so high is they thought we were east coast mobsters, when the truth is, we were just a couple of two-bit criminals trying to make ends meet the hard way.

A tough guy in a tough place

So I ended up in jail awaiting trial, but I wasn't about to stay there. They had these inmates called trustees who had proven they could be trusted by the guards. They had extra privileges and had more contact with outsiders, so I approached one and asked him if he could get a gun for me. I hated being locked up and was prepared to shoot my way out if I had to. The trustee assured me he'd have a gun in my hands the next day, then went straight to a guard. As I was in my cell waiting for the gun, about fifteen guards showed up in full riot gear and with two big ornery-looking German shepherds. I put up a struggle, but I was no match for them. In about two minutes I was in shackles. They carted me off to the old Nashville Metro Workhouse and dumped me in the "hole"—solitary confinement in a windowless fortress about the size of a closet.

Finally, my trial date rolled around. I knew I'd be found guilty, which I was. The only thing that interested me was the time I'd have to do. I suppose I should have been happy with the fifteen year sentence, since earlier I'd been offered a plea bargain for sixty years. But the thought of spending the next fifteen years of my life behind bars hit me between the eyes like a brick. And when I learned my new address, the reality sunk in: Tennessee State Penitentiary, fondly known as "The Walls." If you've ever seen the movie, "The Green Mile" with Tom Hanks, you've seen my new home. Designed for 800 men, when I arrived, there were 1,600 guys crammed like sardines behind its three-foot thick stone walls guarded by gun turrets. It was a tough place, but I was a tough guy. At least I thought I was. I had to be. The fact of the matter was I was also scared.

That's just the way it is when you grow up being told you're nothing but a piece of white trash.

2

We Don't Want Your Kind Here

I never knew my parents.

Apparently my father was a merchant marine who was always on a ship somewhere. My mom? I have no recollection of her, but my best guess is that without a husband around it was just too much for her to look after my brother and sister and me. My first memory of family is an orphanage in Portland, Oregon. Thankfully, orphanages are a relic of the past, having been replaced by the much more humane (at least for the most part) system of foster care. But back in the 1950's, just about every city in America had an orphanage for kids nobody wanted.

I was one of those kids.

I'm sure most of the folks at my orphanage were motivated by genuine compassion for kids like us, but all I remember of the place was that you mostly had to fend for yourself. I don't recall anyone holding me on their lap or reading me bedtime stories. If I got sick, no one sat by my bed and put a cool cloth to my forehead or told me I would be okay. You just gutted it out and tried to stay out of trouble. Every now and then the older boys would get into fights, which was exciting but also scary. And they must not have been regulated because if you got out of line, they'd give you a whippin'. I guess they never got the memo that corporal punishment to that extreme was child abuse.

One day my brother, sister, and I got called down to the office. Usually that meant we'd done something wrong, but when we got to the office, we were introduced to a young woman who said she was related to us. Her mom, she said, was our Aunt Millie—our father's half-sister—and she had come to take us to live with her. We kids never knew we had any relatives, so this was a big day for us. I have no idea how they cut through all the red tape that must have been necessary to send three kids off with a perfect stranger, but within a few hours we were on a plane. After a long day of travel we found ourselves in Wauchula, a small town in central Florida with the distinction of being called the "Cucumber Capital of the World."

I know I should have been happy to finally have a family of sorts, and initially I was. But it wasn't long before I began to wonder if being part of a step-family is any better than being stuck in an orphanage. Aunt Millie was a good woman; a hard-working, no nonsense country woman. She meant well, and she must have had a good heart to take in three orphans at her age. No doubt it was too much for her. I don't know how many times she told me I'd end up like my father, "a no good bum," as she put it. I hated hearing that. What boy wants to have those kinds of thoughts of a father he never knew? I'm sure she believed that reminding me just how bad I could turn out would make me want to try harder to be good, but all it did was make me angry. I appreciate that she felt a certain obligation to look after her half-brother's children, but she didn't make us feel welcome. A woman of humble means, she constantly reminded us that we ate too much, taxing her limited grocery budget. I'm sure she didn't mean for us to feel this way, but we got the clear impression that our presence in her life created hardships that did not exist before our arrival. My reaction to feeling so unwanted?

I ran away. I continued to run away, even after being caught a number of times.

Doing time at ten years old

Today, if a kid runs away from home, he gets picked up, brought back to his parents, and they hopefully will receive family counseling. In 1956, they put me in a "reformatory," which for all practical purposes was a prison for kids.

It's pretty accurate to say I began doing time when I was ten years old, carted off to the Florida State Reform School in Okeechobee, Florida—some eighty miles southeast of Wauchula.

In some ways, I thought the reformatory was a good deal: three squares a day, got to meet a lot of other kids, and no one to tell me I would never amount to much. During the day we went to school, then at night we bunked in dormitories—about forty kids to a dorm. They also put us to work during our spare time: cleaning toilets, doing dishes, or raking the grounds. I didn't mind the work, and I did well in school, so overall I really didn't mind being there.

The goal was to "reform" you. But, just like in prison, you simply learn the fine art of breaking all the rules. Unfortunately, if you got caught, the reformatory wasn't a great place to be. One of the times I broke a rule, I got caught by a "counselor," and he took me to a room with six or seven grown men who held me down over a bunk. Then one of the guys whipped my rear end with something called a razor strop—a wide piece of leather used to put a nice edge on a barber's straight razor. They attached that leather strop to a wooden handle for better leverage and did their best to beat out of me whatever caused me to break the rules.

I did my time there as a ten-year old criminal: one year. But when I was returned home, things didn't get any better for me. One of the downsides of small towns is that everybody knows each other's business. I was the kid who got sent to the reformatory, the kid who had no parents, the kind of kid nice families didn't want their children to play with. And if I couldn't quite figure that out on my own, there were plenty of people around to spell it out for me in plain English.

One day I was sitting with a few other kids in a little community center in town, ironically a place for youngsters to hang out and stay out of trouble. The high school football coach walked into the community center and made a beeline for me at the table where I was talking to some other kids.

"What are you doing here?" he asked in that tone of voice that told me I wasn't being recruited for the football team.

I was embarrassed, confused, and unsure of what to say. I mean, this was a place for kids to hang out. I was just starting to make some friends, and I really wanted to fit in.

Before I could answer he said, "We don't want your kind in here."

Words matter

It's amazing how a word or two from a prominent adult can influence the trajectory of a child's life. In some small towns the football coach ranks somewhere between the President of the United States and God. I had tasted the insanity of institutionalization and was trying to enter the more appealing world of conformity and respectability, and this high priest of sport publicly banished me from the world I so desperately wanted to join.

He reaffirmed what I had begun to conclude all along: I wasn't much. I had no parents, no family, no friends, no support. If I was going to make it in this harsh and unfriendly world, I'd better start watching out for myself.

So I did.

This was the heart of the deep south, and in those days just about every town, big or small, had a white section and a black section. Only the black section was called the "colored" side of town or "N" Quarters. The white folks pretty much stayed on their side of town and the black folks stayed on theirs. If you were white, you could go anywhere you wanted in town, but if you were black and wandered over into the white side of town, you did so at your own risk. It's just the way it was back then.

But maybe because they knew what it was like to be ostracized, I always got along well with the black folks. I started a "business" with them. I'd steal cartons of cigarettes in a little grocery store on my side of town, then go over to their side of town and sell them to my black friends. And though it was a way for a kid to put a little money in his wallet, they were more than just customers to me. They invited me into their homes, fed me, and totally accepted me. Something my own people didn't do.

Things were going pretty well in my business. I was making money and I enjoyed being around people who seemed to like me. Then I got busted for stealing the cigarettes. Now I was living proof that the reformatory didn't quite reform me. They sent me back to Okeechobee to finish what they were unable to do the first time. Only this time, the concept of "foster care" was beginning to catch on, so after I was sufficiently reformed—another year of learning the ropes from other like-minded kids and taking a few beatings along the way—they sent me to a family who had agreed to take me in as their own. I'm sure these were nice people who wanted to help a young kid who was heading down the wrong path, but by now I was what they called "incorrigible." It wasn't just others who thought that about me; it's how I had begun to think of myself. I concluded there was something wrong with me because I didn't have what the other kids had: a family, love, and security.

I also started thinking I was a tough guy. One thing you learn in reform school is to take care of yourself, mostly because no one else will. And if that means not backing down when another guy challenges you, well, you make sure the other guy and everyone else knows you aren't afraid of fighting. I was in my share of fights, so by the time I got back home, I was the guy nobody messed with, and I liked the "respect" it earned me. In addition to being the tough guy, however, I wanted to show people I wasn't all brawn and no brain. I kept hearing Aunt Millie telling me I'd end up just like my dad, so I worked hard in school to prove I wasn't dumb. I'd kept up with my schooling inside the reformatory, so when I got back into the public school I did very well. In fact, I was actually a good student, but that didn't seem to make any difference. Not to my teachers, not to anyone. I was still this kid with no parents who now had two stints at the reformatory. If I was going to make it, I'd have to get out of this town.

Escape!

One day I was walking down the main drag in town and saw a car parked alongside the street with its windows open and the keys in the ignition. In those days, people often left their homes and cars unlocked, so this in itself wasn't unusual. But at that moment, those keys looked like my ticket out of there. My younger brother, Phillip, was with me, so I nudged him and nodded in the direction of the car and asked, "Whadda ya think?"

He smiled and said, "Sure!"

Just like that, we were in the car and heading north. We had absolutely no idea where we were going, only what we were getting away from. We got about thirty miles out of town when the reality of what we had done sank in: the gas gauge was on empty. No problem. I pulled into the next gas station, filled up the tank, then got back into the car and pulled back onto the highway. As far as I knew, the old guy behind the counter either never saw us or figured it would be too much of a hassle to call the police. Anyway, we got away with it, and a few hours later when we were close to being out of gas again, I knew exactly what to do. I did this a few times until we were close to Aiken, South Carolina. The next station, however, was a little more savvy than the previous ones. As I sped off, confident that we'd just gotten another free tank of gas, I glimpsed something in the rear-view mirror that quickly wiped the smile off my face: three cars pulling out of the gas station and closing ground between us.

The chase was on. I stomped on the accelerator, gaining a little distance on them, but the next time I looked in the mirror, I saw another car had joined the chase—this one had red and blue lights flashing. I had just turned sixteen and did not have much driving experience, but I managed to keep the posse at bay for several miles. By now we were just outside of Aiken, and I figured we had a chance to ditch them for good. We were doing around a hundred miles an hour after rounding a wide bend, where for a brief second or two we were out of their line of sight. I tried to make a quick turn down a side road to evade them, but the car skidded wildly through the intersection before crashing into an embankment. Within seconds we were surrounded by about six angry men and a couple of cops with their guns drawn.

They let my brother off because of his age—he was only fifteen—and because they felt he was influenced by me, which he was. But I wasn't so lucky. Because my crime of stealing a car was a felony, they weren't about to send me back to the reformatory. They threw me in jail in Aiken, put me on trial, and gave me what was called a "zip six" sentence: six months to six years. That in itself was bad enough, but they weren't done with me. Because I had driven the stolen car across state lines, my felony became a federal offense. So instead of serving my time in the relative "comfort" of a South Carolina jail, they sent me off to Washington, D.C.

To one of the toughest, meanest, integrated prisons in America for youthful offenders.

3

A Bad, Bad Place

When the prison bus stopped in front of the processing center of NTS, short for National Training School for Boys, I had no idea what I was in for. By now I had spent about two and a half years in the reformatory in Okeechobee and several weeks in the city jail in Aiken, South Carolina, and thought this was just another lock-up. While I never liked the idea of being incarcerated, I'd learned how to get along: mind your own business and if someone challenges you, don't back down.

But this place was unlike any other lockup I had experienced. For one thing, there were two distinct prison populations: federal prisoners and D.C. prisoners, or just "DC's." The federal prisoners were like me— youthful offenders between the ages of fifteen and eighteen who had committed felonies. But the DC's were all residents of the District who had committed felonies. For whatever reason, the age limit for the DC's was twenty one.

Oh, and another thing: the federals were white and the DC's were black.

This little fact meant absolutely nothing to me except that maybe I'd have friends inside. The only people who'd been decent to me up until then were the blacks who lived on the other side of the tracks. My own "kind" pretty much let me know they didn't want me around, so I was fine hanging out with black people. Even though the Deep South was so tragically segregated at that time, there was a quiet understanding blacks and whites had with each other: you stay on your side of town, we'll stay on ours, and we'll get along just fine. And we did, for the most part. We coexisted peacefully, though the blacks always got the short end of the stick.

But to borrow from Dorothy in "The Wizard of Oz," I wasn't in the south anymore.

I was now in what was considered to be the north, and the black men I encountered in this prison hated whites in general, but they despised white boys from the south in particular. To them, I was "the man"— the privileged white kid whose parents or grandparents were slave owners living on vast plantations built on the backs of black people. For the first time in my life I understood what it was like to be hated just for the color of your skin, something these guys had known all their lives. I also experienced what it was like to be a minority, because at this particular prison, the blacks outnumbered the whites by about six to one.

I had never seen hatred like that in my life, especially from black people. I realize I had been blind to the way blacks had been treated in America. I was too busy running away from home or trying to avoid beatings in the reformatory to know about places like Selma, Alabama. Being from the south, it's a pretty safe bet that our white school teachers never filled us in on the lynchings or church bombings that the blacks had to contend with in neighboring states. The first time a black guy threatened to kill me at this prison I wanted to say, "Hey—you got the wrong guy. Whitey has treated me the same way he's treated you." But of course, despite all I had to put up with from my own people, I had something these guys didn't have: white skin. And to them, that made me the enemy.

For the next two and a half years, I was the enemy.

Armed and dangerous

I thought I was a tough guy, but I'll be honest. The whole time I was in that place I was scared. I saw stuff no human being should see in a lifetime. The place was overcrowded, dirty, and violent. I later learned that the United States Attorney General closed the place down. His name was Bobby Kennedy.

Nearly every day a fight would break out, and it was always the same—a white guy and a black guy would walk past each other and the next thing you know, fists were flying. It was always fast and furious, with usually three or four more black guys jumping on the white guy. About once a week an "ordinary" fight would erupt into the closest thing to a riot I ever want to see. You'd be sitting at a table in the mess hall—blacks on one side, whites on the other—and almost as if someone gave a signal, literally all heck would break loose. By the time the guards got things settled down, there were usually a dozen or so guys on the floor lying in a pool of their own blood. NTS was a bad, bad place, and like the reformatory, it did nothing to reform me. If anything, it taught me to be a better criminal. And it filled me with hate.

Toward the end of my time, however, I got into a mentorship program. A man named Frederick Oechsner became not only my mentor but my friend. At first I saw him as just another do-gooder who had nothing better to do, but after I got out I learned he was a prominent journalist with the Associated Press and an author who had interviewed Hitler four times prior to World War II. A classy guy. Once a week he drove from his office in Washington, D.C. to NSB, where he met with me in a visitors' area to encourage me and try to point me in the right direction. After I was released, he bought me my first suit and treated me to my first steak dinner ever.

Transformed by hatred

But Mr. Oechsner's efforts weren't enough. That prison had transformed me all right. I left there filled with rage and hatred. I hated the black man, hated the rich man, hated anyone who seemed to have it better than me, and that was pretty much everyone. I don't like to admit it, but the hatred I witnessed in that prison rubbed off on me in a big way. We were all powerless; society's rejects. I may have left that place a free man, but in reality I was a slave to my hatred and resentment.

I had no place to go, so I caught a bus heading south and eventually made my way back to the only place I knew. But if I was every parent's nightmare as a fourteen-year-old reformatory kid, you can imagine what they thought of an eighteen-year-old just getting out of federal prison. It was clear there was no future there, so I headed off to Tampa where I got a job with Florida Steel. After lugging heavy steel bars around for a few weeks, I finally got a letter from an uncle who said he really wanted me.

His name was Sam, as in Uncle Sam, as in "You've just been drafted into the United States Army."

Since Wauchula was the county seat of Hardee County, I didn't have far to travel to get to the county building, where I boarded a bus with about thirty other guys my age. Nine hours later we rolled into Fort Jackson, South Carolina, where it became obvious this wasn't going to be summer camp. When they opened the bus door, it was what you see in the movies: a haphazard, rag-tag bunch of nervous-looking guys marching toward a nondescript building while a drill sergeant screams insults at you the whole way. Then the haircut, ten-second physical, and more screaming as you pull on an ill-fitting uniform and lace up your boots. Welcome to the United States Army!

Finally, a family

The entire eight to ten weeks of basic training we did nothing but carry sixty-pound backpacks up a torture chamber affectionately called "Drag Hill." It didn't matter if you were going to the rifle range, parade grounds, or mess hall—the route always managed to take you up this steep hill that was nearly impossible to climb without stopping to catch your breath. But stopping for even a second gave the drill sergeant occasion to scream at you louder and send you back down to climb it again.

It was tough, but I can't say I complained much. In fact, I rather enjoyed it. For the first time in my life I felt as if I belonged. In some ways, being in the Army was like having a family, something I had never had. Most of the kids who got drafted were like me. In those days you could get a deferment for going to college, but none of us could afford college. For the most part, we were just a bunch of poor whites and blacks. So I got along with the guys and felt as if I were improving myself. And one thing the Army is good at is putting structure into your life. There was no time to waste because every second of your day was planned. And it was the same every day. You got up at 5:00 and had exactly five minutes to get dressed, make your bed (and yes—so flat and tight the drill sergeant could bounce a quarter off it), and stand for inspection. Then it was a fast march in formation to the mess hall, where you could eat all you wanted in the five minutes they gave you. The rest of the day was filled with drills, instructions screamed at you, and always a few trips up that hated hill before you finally collapsed onto your bed at lights out. Even if you wanted to sneak off and party somewhere, you couldn't. You were just too dang tired. Then bright and early the next morning you had the pleasure of doing it all over again.

Being ordered around and pushed to do things that seemed impossible didn't sit well with some of my buddies, but for me, it felt good. For the first time in my life, I was actually gaining self-confidence and becoming proud of myself. It didn't happen often, but to hear even just once a nasty, ornery drill sergeant say, "Nice job, Carlson," was music to my ears. It's funny, but when all your life you've been told you're a loser and you'll never amount to anything, even the faintest praise is a huge motivator. It made me want to work harder, learn more, and become an even better soldier.

After basic training I moved on to AIT, or Advanced Infantry Training. The infantry are the grunts on the ground in a war—the guys who shoot and get shot at. We got plenty of practice at both, including crawling through mud with live ammo whizzing over our heads by about six inches. There was no room for error, and it was a great way to teach you to keep your head down.

I hadn't paid much attention to what was going on in the world, but the whole purpose of all this training was to prepare us to go to war. This being 1969, the war they were preparing us for was in the tiny country of Vietnam. In 1969, 11, 616 American soldiers were killed in Vietnam, the second highest number of American deaths of any year in that war. Once I realized I'd probably end up there, I took my training even more seriously. I wasn't especially afraid—when you're barely twenty-two years old, you're invincible. Or so you think. But I was smart enough to know that I'd fare better if I was properly prepared. I'll say this for all the structure and discipline dished out by the drill sergeants and instructors—by the time they were done with you, you were a man. When I first got there, I thought I was a tough guy, and in a way I was. But the Army channeled all that toughness and hatred, and I was transformed into a young soldier who was ready and equipped to fight for his country, not just for himself.

Sure enough, we got our orders and mine said "Vietnam." Normally when you finish your training, you get a two-week leave before you head off to your next duty, but for guys going to Vietnam, they gave you thirty days: enough time to get your affairs in order. So I had a full month before I needed to report to Fort Lewis near Seattle, where I would join my unit, board a military jet, and head over the Pacific to Saigon. Since I had no place else to go, I figured I'd go back to Wauchula and hang out for the month. I was sitting on my bunk packing my gear into a big olive-green duffel bag when the drill sergeant leaned into the doorway of our barracks.

"Carlson, report to the CQ asap!" he barked. I smiled to myself. Even getting rid of us didn't seem to make him happy.

CQ, or Charge of Quarters, was basically the front gate of the fort, and guys who pull that duty are the ones who take phone calls from the outside. I was a little curious because being called to CQ usually meant you had a message, and I had no idea who would be trying to contact me. During my whole time at basic training and AIT, I don't recall receiving a letter from anyone.

So I dropped what I was doing and headed over to CQ to see what was up.

When I walked into the office, a guy behind a desk pointed to the phone and said, "Carlson, your mother's on the phone."

"You've got the wrong guy, bud," I said as I turned to head back to my barracks. "My mother's dead."

"Look, there's a lady on the phone who says she's your mother and she's crying. The least you can do is talk to her."

Reluctantly, I picked up the phone.

4

Goodbye Mom, Hello Vietnam

Back when I lived in the orphanage in Portland, Oregon, like any kid I was curious about my parents. When I asked one of the adults where my mom and dad were, she told me both of them had died and that's why I was sent to the orphanage. Since I had no memory of them, I can't say the news about their deaths had much of an impact on me. It was sort of like learning about the death of a second-cousin you never knew you had. It went in one ear and out the other and I got back to whatever I was doing.

So when the guy at CQ told me my mom was on the phone, I knew it was a mistake. I honestly didn't want to talk to whoever was on the other end of the line. I wasn't even curious. And I wasn't pleased to be the one to tell her she had the wrong guy. But I picked up the phone.

At first, I couldn't understand a word she was saying because she was crying hysterically. But I knew something was up because I heard her say my name a few times between sobs. She finally calmed down enough to convince me she really *was* my mom. All those years, everyone had lied to me. The folks at the orphanage, everyone.

What do you do when for years you believed you were an orphan only to learn it wasn't true? I was stunned. I was shocked to discover my mom was really alive, and I didn't know what to say. She asked me how I was and what I was doing, and when I told her I was about to ship out to Vietnam, she started crying again. In her mind, I was still her baby and she knew that guys who go over there sometimes return in a flag-draped coffin. She told me she was living in Oregon and wondered if I would visit her before I left. Almost without thinking, I told her I would. She gave me her address, and just like that, the first conversation I ever had with my mother was over.

A bittersweet reunion

Oregon was just next door to Washington, where I'd be shipping out, so it would be easy to pay her a visit. To this day, I have no idea how she tracked me down. This was before the internet, so she must have worked pretty hard. On my end, I wasn't sure what to think. Of course there was a part of me that was elated. Who wouldn't be? After all these years of feeling alone and out of place because I didn't have a real family, I was excited to meet her; learn more about what happened. But there's a part of me that tapped into a bedrock of anger I'd carried around with me. What exactly *did* happen? What was it about us that caused her to abandon us to an orphanage? Why couldn't she have tracked us down when we were younger and desperately needed a mother to love and care for us?

I got off the plane in Portland and rented a car to drive the thirty miles or so to her house. From the looks of it, she hadn't had an easy life. The place was run down and in one of those neighborhoods where even the nicer places had "hard times" written all over them. I took a deep breath and knocked on the door.

When I saw the little woman who answered the door, I have to admit, I more or less lost it. And she did too. We cried and held each other as if I were a newborn tucked in close to her in the hospital bed. This was my mother—my real, honest-to-goodness mom. All the emotions of feeling rejected because I didn't have any parents came rushing over me as I held this woman and wondered what might have been if she had raised me, could have read me bedtime stories and taught me my ABC's. I might have been a grown man about to ship out and defend my country, but in that moment I was little Carl holding onto my mother and wishing we could go back to the beginning and start over.

The plan was for me to spend the next two weeks with her, getting caught up on our lives and laying a foundation for moving forward. After all I'd been through, I desperately just wanted to be "normal," whatever that was. In the back of my mind, I was thinking how cool it would be to get back from Vietnam and find this woman who loved me. Then I would start a family, and watch my mom be the grandma to them that I never had. The Army had begun to reshape my life—given me a sense of self-worth—and this reunion with my mom planted a seed of hope inside me that maybe, just maybe, things were starting to work out for me.

Then I met Richard.

Apparently my father had died, just like they told me. Mom knew she couldn't give us the kind of home she felt we deserved, so she reluctantly took us to the orphanage, then dropped out of sight. Maybe Aunt Millie and the others thought that telling us she was dead would be easier for us to handle than hearing she handed us over to complete strangers at an orphanage. Somewhere along the way, she married Richard, and they had children together, but it was anything but one big happy family. I sensed right away that this was a hugely dysfunctional family, largely because of Richard.

I was not generally judgmental of others, since I hadn't been a model citizen myself, but Richard was an alcoholic. Not just an alcoholic but the kind we call an "angry drunk." He seemed nice enough when he was sober; it's just that he was hardly ever sober.

When he started drinking—usually shortly after he woke up—he was a holy terror. He'd curse at the kids, and if they were within his reach he'd cuff 'em up the side of the head. He ordered my mom around, and if she didn't do what he said quickly enough, he'd shower her with a string of obscenities. He made it clear he wasn't overjoyed to have me walk into their lives, but that didn't really bother me too much. It wasn't the first time I'd been unwanted.

Things started to get a little tense when one day I told him to knock it off after a particularly harsh brow-beating of my mom. We stood toe-to-toe yelling at each other before Mom got between us. From the bruises on her arms and some discoloration on her forehead, I suspected he didn't just yell at her when he was angry. Sure enough, I heard him shouting at her in the kitchen the next afternoon, and when I walked in to try to calm him down, I saw him hit her. That was it for me. We went at it pretty good, and I probably would have hurt the guy badly were it not for Mom pulling me off and begging me to stop.

I still had about a week before my unit left for Vietnam, but I knew I couldn't stay there. For one thing, I probably *would* have ended up killing Richard. Even though I didn't have a proper upbringing, I knew men do not hit women. Ever. I also realized that my mom, for whatever reason, was willing to put up with

Richard, and I had no intention of sticking around to figure out why.

So, I left that sad and bewildering place. In a few days I was standing on a hot tarmac, sweat-drenched from ninety degree heat and ninety percent humidity.

Vietnam

I learned a number of things while I served my country in the Vietnam War. I served in two different areas. The first was with the 25th Infantry Division, and the second was the 24th Transportation Company. During my time in the 25th I did see some action. We went on what they called "search and destroy" missions, which meant a lot of humping the bush and hunting down the bad guys. There were several fire fights, but that's about it. Most of the time, our efforts were futile. One sure thing about the Vietcong: they were savvy soldiers. They literally disappeared into the jungle, yet we knew they were close by. We set up ambushes, but I don't recall any of them being successful. I earned the CIB, Combat Infantry Badge, which was awarded to men who had experienced combat. The last half of my time there, I was assigned to the 24th Transportation, where I worked a number of different jobs.

The most important lesson I learned in Vietnam came from observing the Vietnamese people. I grew up dirt poor, at least by American standards. But when you see people in the middle of a war, scratching out a desperate living and nearly starving, it moves you. It makes you understand how blessed we who live in America truly are. These people had strength, perseverance, and grit.

A virtual drug store

Vietnam left another impression on me that would haunt me for years: drugs. The place was a virtual drug store. I was a southern country boy, and for me a big time was Saturday night and a couple of beers. But from the moment I stepped off the plane, I was offered just about every drug you could imagine. You name it—Marijuana, Speed, Heroin—it was all there for the taking, and cheap. You didn't have to sneak around to get it or use it. Everybody knew what was going on, from the top down. Our camp had two "hootches," or fortified huts, where you could go to chill out. One was for the "juicers," the guys who liked to drink; the other was for the "heads," the drug users. I frequented both.

Finally, my tour of duty came to an end and I got my orders to report to Fort Dix, New Jersey, where I was encouraged to enter the Drill Sergeant Academy. My mentor was a hard-as-nails Louisiana boy—Bobby Cheetham—who kicked my butt all the way through the course. He had seventeen years in the army, two tours in Vietnam, and as a drill sergeant was as tough a guy as you'll ever find. I owe him big time for pushing me the way he did.

A proud moment

When graduation day came around, we marched into an auditorium filled with people and took our seats up front next to a long table where all the brass and various officers were seated. After a few speeches and other formalities, the commanding general walked up to the podium and began calling out the names of the graduates so each of us could walk across the stage, receive our diplomas, and get our campaign hats—what civilians sometimes refer to as a Smokey the Bear hat. When finally I heard my name called, I walked, shoulders back and chest out in front of all those people. When the general handed me my hat, it was the proudest day of my life. I was a Vietnam veteran and the youngest drill sergeant in the entire battalion. For a brief moment I thought I might make something of my life after all. The greatest thing I learned in the Army was discipline. To this day I have strived to live a disciplined life.

But I was pure crazy.

After I earned my promotion to drill sergeant, I began hanging out with my mentor, Bobby Cheetham, and another drill sergeant, Roy White. We'd work our troops during the day, then three or four times a week head for the bar and drink half the night, only to drag ourselves out of bed at five in the morning to do it all over again. Train troops to go to war, then go out drinking—pretty much the path I chose during the remaining service I owed my country. However, I served this country honorably. I have always believed that the United States of America is the greatest country on earth and worth fighting for. Today the world is a different place than it was then, confronted often with terrorism, against which we must have the moral conviction and resolve to battle any extreme threats. America is still worth fighting for.

The time came for me to make the decision to stay in or leave the Army, and I reluctantly chose to go. Fort Dix was offering job training to all Vietnam veterans, and I signed up to become a bricklayer. They introduced me to a little Italian guy who was a master bricklayer, and he taught me well. I went out and bought a set of brand new trowels and chisels and other bricklaying equipment and was excited about my new career. But like everything else in my life to that point, this optimism was short lived.

The war in Vietnam was winding down, and the economy followed suit. Undaunted, I hit every construction site I could find, trying to land a job. Always, I got one of two answers: "There's no work," or "You don't have enough experience." I kept at it for a month or more, getting turned down probably fifty times before the frustration and disappointment smacked me square in the face. Driving across a bridge one day, after being told one more time there was no work, I stopped in the middle of the bridge and walked around to the back of the car. I opened the trunk where my masonry tools were and in frustration grabbed them and threw them into the river. My career in masonry ended before it was begun.

Thus began my new career: full-time bouncer and part-time crook. In the largest nightclub in southern New Jersey, at a place called Casper's, I was a bouncer. As for my other job, it was arsonist for hire, specializing in jewelry store heists. The money was good, but I went through it like water through a sieve. Chasing women, doing drugs, the good life. Or so I thought. But it was about to all come crashing down on me after that ill-fated robbery in Nashville.

You'd think by the time they threw me into a cell at the Tennessee State Prison—the much-hated "Walls"—I'd come to my senses. But I was buck crazy, and this was just another stop for me on the highway to destruction.

5

There Ain't No God in Here

It didn't take long for me to discover why they described a sentence to Tennessee State Prison as "hard time." Nothing about the place was easy. Its very appearance was designed to strike fear into the hearts of its inmates. It was a fortress-like structure built on the banks of the Cumberland River. When it opened in 1898, its 800 cells were designed for single occupancy. They were not nearly enough to house the 1,600 inmates assigned there. Overcrowding was a critical issue. Each cell was an eight-foot by five-foot tomb wrapped on three sides by thick concrete walls and fronted by steel bars that opened to a narrow catwalk. The comforts of home were packed into that little cell: a rickety bunk with a mattress all of two inches thick, a tiny stainless steel sink with running water—cold and lukewarm, a single overhead light bulb that you couldn't turn on or off (that service was provided by the guards), a small trunk under the bed to store all your possessions, and a toilet. Privacy? Forget about it. Whatever you did in that cell, someone was always watching.

Everything inside was regimented and structured. When the lights came on at six in the morning, you got dressed and waited for your cell door to open so you could march to the mess hall. After breakfast—if you could call it that—you headed off to your work assignment in one of the prison workshops, ostensibly to help pay for the costs of your incarceration. After lunch they let you out in the yard to exercise, which usually meant watching your back. You didn't get sent to this place for parking violations. These were some of the most dangerous criminals in all of Tennessee, and the best way to survive was to never stand down if someone challenged you. If you were a "model prisoner," it usually meant you were a snitch, and snitches seldom lived to see the end of their sentences.

I was not a model prisoner.

Through most of my twenty-six years I'd had to prove myself. I was the kid nobody thought would amount to much, and I pretty much proved them right. Now I had to start over again in my new "home," and I quickly established my reputation as a guy you didn't want to mess with. I figured I had nothing to lose. To a man my age, fifteen years might as well be a life sentence. Good behavior wasn't part of my career plan. The longest I'd ever been locked up was two and a half years in D.C. as a teenager, so by the time I began my fourth year at the prison, I simply accepted the fact that I'd be an old man by the time I got out.

As was the case with most lock-ups, some of the guys would "get religion," which to me was a big joke. I'd never been to church except for a few times as a kid when someone from the community would pick up my brother and sister and me to take us to a little country church outside of town. The only other times were when I was in one of the foster homes. I hated church, not so much because of anything they taught, but because it was in that little church that the choir director, who apparently was trusted by everybody, would take me to the drive-in movies and sexually abuse me. I never wanted anything to do with religion again.

By this time, I had settled into a fairly uneventful routine. Playing cards, hanging out with my boys (every prison has its little groups or gangs, usually based on skin color or nationality), watching TV, or making hootch (you could ferment just about anything, and though it always tasted terrible, it did the trick). I would stare out the window, but I despised going out in the yard and seeing the blue sky, knowing my buddies on the outside were free. I hated the monotonous menial labor in the workshop, reminding me that at one time I was a skilled tradesman, even if nobody wanted me. I especially hated knowing that for the next fifteen years I would have absolutely no say over what I did. Until you've lost your freedom, you don't know how precious it is. When you take away a man's liberty, despair sets in. Fast.

Finally, someone cared about me

One Saturday, sometime during my fourth year in prison, a guard showed up at my cell.

"Carlson," he barked. "You've got a visitor." It was eerily reminiscent of the time the CQ at Fort Jackson told me my mom was on the phone.

"You've got the wrong guy, man. Ain't no one I know who'd wanna see me." Which was true. I hadn't had a single visitor in the four years I'd been locked up in that place. Not a single letter or message. As far as I was concerned, not a single soul outside gave a darn about me.

"He says he's your brother. Either get your butt out here or I'll tell the guy to get lost. Your call."

I could hardly remember the last time I'd seen Phillip. After I nearly got him arrested for our stolen car caper fourteen years earlier, we lost touch with each other. I'd heard through the grapevine that he'd had a few run-ins with the police, which didn't surprise me. Like it or not, we were what they called "white trash." It's a hard label to shake.

"Okay boss," I shrugged to the guard. "Beats sittin' here waiting for Happy Hour."

In a matter of minutes I was sitting in the visitors' area of the prison, across from the brother I hadn't seen in years. He looked good. In fact, he looked better than I ever remembered him.

"How ya doin' little brother?" I asked.

For the next ten minutes or so we filled each other in on the last several years of our lives. I told him about meeting our mom and of my tour of duty in Vietnam. He told me he'd gotten his life turned around and found a good job. Things were great for him, which pleased me. He was my kid brother; I hadn't been the best influence on him, so to hear that his life was moving in the right direction relieved me. I was glad to learn that I hadn't completely messed up his life.

Then he hit me with something I wasn't prepared for.

"Carl, the reason things are so much better for me now is that I've turned my life over to Jesus Christ. I accepted him as my Lord and Savior."

He might as well have smacked me over the head with a two-by-four. I couldn't believe my ears. Jesus? I'd seen guys who turned to Jesus in prison, and I wanted nothing to do with them. Whenever anyone mentioned Jesus, I thought of that church from my childhood and the two-faced choir director who made such a big deal about how he loved Jesus. No thanks.

I could feel my throat tighten as I responded to my brother's infatuation with Jesus.

"You see these walls, Phillip?" I asked. "You see those gun towers? Do you have any idea what it's like in this hole? There ain't no God in here."

He nodded his understanding, then respectfully explained to me the plan of salvation. He told me how accepting Jesus into his heart had changed his life. I listened with a hardened heart, but I listened. We changed the subject, and eventually our time together was up. My brother put his hand against mine in the prison farewell tradition. And then he left.

As I walked back to my cell, my mind swirled. I detested the whole religion thing. It just seemed like an easy cop-out. Guys who had some sort of conversion experience inside the prison tended to get treated a lot better by the authorities—sometimes getting early releases. The way I looked at it, they used religion to get a better deal. I wasn't thrilled about my sentence, but I wasn't about to cop to a conversion experience just to get out sooner.

And yet I had seen something in my brother's eyes. He had been brought up like me. Dirt poor. Abandoned by our parents. We both had it pounded into our heads that we would never amount to anything, yet here he was with a hope for the future. Hope was clearly something I didn't have, and frankly, I didn't think it was possible for people like us. Still, I couldn't shake the fact that something had happened with Phillip to give him what I had never experienced: contentment. He wasn't the same brother I had known. He had a clear sense of purpose for his life. You could see it in his eyes; hear it in his voice.

By the time I got back to my cell, I told myself that whatever had happened to Phillip was okay for him, but I'd take my chances believing in nothing. I figured it was probably easy to believe in a god when things were going your way, but I really meant what I had said: Why would God waste his time in a place like this?

The crushing weight of my sin

About a year later I was sitting in my cell doing what I did most of the time: nothing. Never one to feel sorry for myself, for the first time since I entered that prison I fought back a growing sense of sadness that was like a giant wave breaking over me. It was as if I finally realized how much I was missing. Most guys my age had gotten married, started families, bought houses. They went to work every day and came home to a wife and kids— maybe went to a Little League game or a school play. Not only did I have none of that, I most likely never would. I was thirty-one years old. By the time I got out I'd be a forty-one year old ex-con, and the world would feel the same way about me that the old football coach had: we don't want your kind around here.

I remembered how I had felt when all those construction sites turned me down, realizing that adding "felon" to my resume pretty much ruined any chance of landing a decent job. And what woman would want to take a middle-aged ex-con home to meet her parents? I felt like giving up, but there was nothing to give up. I'd already lost it all. I was in a bad place, and I didn't know what to do about it. I was about to roll back on my bunk and try to sleep off this uncharacteristic bout of depression when I found myself doing something I had never done in my life.

I cried out to God.

In that cramped, miserable cell in a dangerous penitentiary, for the first time in my life, I prayed the only prayer anyone had ever taught me. It was the sinner's prayer my brother Phillip had given me those many months before.

I didn't even know who God was. I had never believed in him; never wanted to. The only gods in my world were booze and drugs, money, women, and fast cars. As a free man, that's all I had lived for because there was nothing else. If you had asked anyone in that prison who was the most unlikely guy to turn to God, many would have pointed to me. I had never read the Bible and had only reluctantly gone to church a few times because someone dragged me there. I had never heard anyone sing Jesus Loves Me, and no one, except for my brother on our last visit, had ever told me they loved me. Yet now I absolutely knew, and there was no doubt, that I was loved by God. He was right there with me. And I was instantly and forever changed.

At that moment, I knew there was a God and that He had "touched me." I knew he existed. More importantly, I knew he loved me! And I haven't been the same since.

You might think I asked God to get me out of prison after that, but I didn't. I never once prayed to get out of there. Instead, I began asking him for a Godly wife. I promised him, "If you will give me a Christian wife one day (and please, Lord, could you make her pretty, too?), I will serve you the best way I know how for the rest of my life."

6

And She's Pretty Too

Within six months of my encounter with God, he walked me right out of that prison a free man. Much of it had to do with overcrowding and the fact that I'd managed to keep my nose clean for five years—at least that's what they told me. But I know my unexpected freedom came from the God who usually goes to work on people when they give up trying to be their own god.

I gave up big time.

One of the terms of my release was that I had to report to a halfway house. I had no idea what I was going to do beyond that except to serve God somehow. He did such a number on me that all my priorities were rearranged. When I had tried to bust out of that jail in Nashville, it was because I wanted to get back to the things that mattered to me—the wild life. The sole motivating factor in my life was to have a good time.

Now the only thing that mattered was serving God, and I realized that to do that I would need a college education. My options were a bit limited by the fact that I was tied to a halfway house. For the next few years I'd have to stick close to Nashville. When I mentioned all this to my parole officer, he told me about a place called Trevecca Nazarene College (later to become a university) on Murfreesboro Road. I had no idea what a Nazarene was and even less of a clue what Trevecca stood for, but I was about to find out. With the help of the G.I. Bill, I enrolled there, a thirty-two year old freshman with a criminal record longer than most of the professors' resumes.

Not your typical Christian college student

I didn't realize it at the time, but I was a major piece of work for them. When it came to Christianity, I didn't know the difference between a protestant and a catholic. I'd never heard the word evangelical, didn't know the words to "How Great Thou Art," and had never read a book by James Dobson, Charles Swindoll, or Charles Stanley. I was a chain smoker on a campus that didn't allow smoking, and I enjoyed a cold beer in the afternoons.

But man, did those people embrace me. In particular, Dr. John Chilton, Everett Holmes, and Bill Calkin. From my first days there, they demonstrated God's love to me. Not once did they make me feel like an outsider because I didn't grow up in their denomination or an outcast because I'd done time. They welcomed me as they did every new student and made me feel like I belonged. When all your life you've been made to feel you're not wanted, do you know what it means when people treat you like you're one of them? It had a huge impact on me and made me want to do the best I could to convince them their faith in me was not misplaced. Trevecca Nazarene University will always have a special place in my heart. Years later, in 2008, they would bestow on me a great honor, presenting me with an Honorary Doctorate Degree for my nearly thirty years of ministry. But this was still 1980.

Why I loved the library

I attacked my studies with a vengeance. In a way, I had an advantage over the younger students. Being older and having lived through so many difficult experiences, I was serious about my education. It was going to be hard enough to get a job as an ex-con, so I wanted to get the best grades possible to override that blemish on my resume. In other words, I worked extremely hard. I never skipped class, and when I wasn't in class I was in the library.

That's where I first saw her.

I looked up from my studies one afternoon and glimpsed a vision walking past. My heart went, "Pow!" and I was done-for. She was the prettiest girl I had ever seen. I'd been studying before, but that was no longer possible. Who could concentrate? I couldn't even think straight. I only knew one thing, and it was that I had to get to know her. So, I did what any red-blooded American fellow would do: I kept going to the library.

Sometimes she would see me, and we would smile at each other, but then I noticed that she smiled at everybody. Once in a lucky while, I would see her in other places, such as the student center, or in chapel, or on one of the campus sidewalks. Whenever I said hello, she would say it back to me. This was good. This was encouraging. But I had yet to actually meet her.

One day I saw her talking to a girl I had in one of my classes, whose name was Dorothy Henderson (Strong). After class I asked Dorothy about "that girl," and she told me her name was Karen Brown and they were roommates in a little house off campus. She said Karen was a part-time student, working full-time in Trevecca's Development Office. And she informed me of the most important thing of all: Karen was single. That's all I really needed to know, and I decided I was going to ask her out. However, deciding to ask a girl out and actually doing it are two different things. I told myself all the reasons she'd say no: I was at least ten years older than she probably was; she was so beautiful she could have any guy on campus; and once she found out about my past, I'd be history—as had happened with one of the other girls I had dated. Why bother starting something I already knew would end badly?

Then again, what was the worst that could happen? If she was as nice as she seemed, at least she'd let me down easy. After a few days of going back and forth, I finally talked myself into it, and I made my way across campus and up the three flights of stairs to where Karen worked. I met a few people I knew along the way, but I could barely acknowledge them. My heart was racing wildly. And suddenly, there she was. When she saw me, she smiled, as she always did. I knew by now that she was just a friendly person; I understood it wasn't just me, but I liked to believe she smiled a little brighter for me. I introduced myself to her, and we spoke for a bit about… who knows what? I'm sure she must have been wondering about this unexpected visit from a fellow with no apparent administrative business.

I was keeping her from her work, so I finally got down to it and asked her if she'd like to have coffee or lunch one day. No doubt she was taken aback by that, but she kindly said, "Oh, that would be nice." I was on a roll now, so I ventured, "Well, I have these two tickets to the Barn Dinner Theatre if you'd like to have dinner instead." And she said, "I'd really like that." I don't know what we said after that; I don't remember leaving the administration building that day. All that registered in my happy heart was that the prettiest girl in the world was going on a date. With me.

The play was a comedy—and a particularly silly one—which kept the evening light and fun, as a first date should be. The meal was delicious, and we had a truly good time, with laughter and easy conversation. We hit it off, and the next week we went to dinner again. After that, we would take walks together, go to the park, and just talk and get to know each other. I got to know her, anyway. I learned she was a third-generation Nazarene, her father had been Sunday School superintendent in her home church of Sanford, Florida, and her mother sang in the choir and worked with the pre-schoolers. Karen herself just really loved the Lord. I had never known another Christian girl, and I certainly had never known anyone else like her. I knew everything I needed to know about her.

But she knew nothing, really, about me.

I had to tell her the truth

Those first few days were wonderful, but I was going to have to be honest with Karen about my past. I had told her the basic general stuff, and I never lied to her; I just hadn't told her everything. How could I? She knew about my shattered childhood and that I had served honorably in Vietnam. She knew I was a new Christian and had not lived an entirely honorable life before getting saved. I was deliberating on why that wasn't enough. I was certain if she knew about my days of crime and my years in prison she'd see me very differently. I wrestled with my conscience for a little while longer, but I knew the truth would come out eventually, and better now than later.

Karen's 23rd birthday arrived, and I took her to The Fifth Quarter Restaurant, our favorite steakhouse. We had a delicious meal, and I gave her a little gold necklace. I suppose you could say I was softening her up, but honestly, I was already in love with her, and I would have given her the moon if I could. I had to tell her, and now was the time.

So, I did. I laid it all out there... every last thing: my life in the fast lane, my criminal past, and my time in prison. The old shame crept back into my spirit as I relived those years, and I wondered why I'd ever even asked this innocent girl out to begin with. She was stunned, just as any decent young woman would be. But she was kind. She even appeared to be understanding. But that didn't mean she would want to keep spending time with me. I returned to the halfway house, and she drove home. I would find out later that she drove far beyond Nashville, thinking, praying, and wondering what in the world to do.

When she got back to her little house on Nance Lane, she walked next door to talk these things over with her best friend, Melody Cornett (Phillips), and Melody's mother, Gladys. Lucky for me, these are two amazing Christian women who told Karen to pray and fast and seek the Lord's direction.

For the next several days Karen and I did not see each other. I think, actually, we were probably avoiding each other. She didn't know what to say to me, and I didn't want to hear a "Dear John" speech. We would certainly be going our separate ways; I just didn't know exactly when.

Finally, she called me and said, "Let's meet for coffee at Shoney's." Her voice was light, and I couldn't help but be hopeful, yet still I was anxious. When I saw her, she smiled, and no coffee had ever tasted so good! We made small talk for a few minutes, and then she began, "Let's just give this thing a shot, why don't we? We'll be friends for awhile, getting to know each other better, then see what happens. I think you're a really great guy… and believe it or not," she added with a wink, "I'm just a sinner myself, saved by God's grace."

This amazing girl, who was working her way through college, who was so pretty she could have any guy she wanted, and who had left home at eighteen to attend a Christian college in another state, had just learned she was dating a man who had been in prison. And she didn't mind being seen with him.

Yep, miracles happen.

Crazy little thing called love

From that point on, though we tried to "be friends for awhile," we grew closer and closer. We studied together when we could, ate lunch together every day, and made time for more dates. We went horseback riding, bowling, and I taught her how to play pool. We swam in my apartment pool and grilled out with friends. We also went to church together. I snuck a kiss whenever I could, and we held hands wherever we went... like teenagers.

Karen's parents drove up from Florida that summer, and we spent an entire Saturday at Percy Warner Park, hiking, playing Frisbee, picnicking, and talking. I genuinely liked Vernon and Frances Brown. I also got to know Karen's brothers, Michael (Micky) and Jeff. They all treated me as well as Karen did, and I became acquainted with the kind of family I had never known before.

Karen told me later that her father had never particularly cared for a single fellow she had ever dated; not because they were bad guys, just never good enough for his only daughter. For him to like me as much as he did astonished her. But of course, he knew nothing of my past. That day was looming....

As I mentioned earlier, I was already in love with Karen, and the dream was growing in my heart of marrying her. I hadn't told her any of this yet because I didn't want her to think I was crazy, moving so fast. Within a few weeks, though, I began to suspect she was feeling the same way, so I gathered my courage and told her I loved her. She thrilled my heart by saying she loved me too. Musicians sing about it and poets write about it, but it's really true. There's no greater feeling than falling in love—especially for a guy who had not known love for the first thirty-three years of his life. I knew that Karen liked me—why else would she want to spend time with me? But love? That's a different story. Suddenly I wanted to be an even better person and to never let her down.

First comes love, then comes . . .

Waiting any longer wouldn't do. I made reservations for two at Kobe's Japanese Steakhouse, a place neither of us had ever been, but had talked about. I made a legal trip to a jewelry store, and with Karen's roommate Dorothy's help, came up with a plan to propose to the lady I loved so much. Dorothy invited her boyfriend, Duane, and the four of us spent a fun-filled day at Opryland, Nashville's premier amusement park. Afterward, Karen and Dorothy went back to their house, and I went home to change for our dinner date. Dorothy told Karen she should put on her prettiest dress, and when I picked her up again, she was glowing; partly from the day's earlier sunshine, but partly, I like to believe, from joy. It was all over her face.

How I delighted to see the sparkle in her eyes as she watched the skilled cooks/entertainers wielding their sharp knives while chopping and grilling our meal in expert showmanship. And oh, how I tensed up at the thought of what was coming next.

After the meal, we went for a walk in the moonlight and I asked her to marry me. When she said yes, I think the earth actually did move, like they say. Whether or not it did, Karen had just made me the strongest, happiest, most successful man on the planet. The night, weeks prior, when I had told her about my past, I never could have imagined this indescribable moment.

This was the summer of 1980, the best summer of my life. The stars were shining brighter than I had ever noticed before, the sky was clearer... and I'm pretty confident in my belief that the angels were singing.

We were getting married.

My prayer to God in that prison cell had been answered: he had brought me to a beautiful Christian woman, and she was going to be my wife. As I reveled in my fortune, however, stark reality hit me once again. While Karen had said yes, I knew she wouldn't want to get married without her parents' blessing, especially her father's. And while Vernon Brown seemed to like me, he didn't have a clue about my stained and troubled past.

Karen, as it turned out, was calling her parents that same weekend. What would any Godfearing father say to his daughter when she broke the news that she was engaged to an ex-felon?

7

Now What?

We have all boys, so I can't relate to a dad getting a long-distance call from his daughter announcing her marriage plans. I'm sure it came as a surprise to Karen's dad when he got the call, but not nearly as much as the shock that came next:

"Dad," she continued, "There's something else I need to tell you. Carl served five years in prison for armed robbery."

Put yourself in her father's shoes. Probably all his life he prayed that Karen would meet a respectable, young Nazarene boy—maybe a preacher's kid—get married, live in a house with a white picket fence, and someday give him grandchildren. He sends her off to a Nazarene college where only good kids go. He knows he'll one day get "the call." And when he does, his daughter tells him she is marrying an ex-con.

Which makes my soon-to-be father-in-law's response astounding to me. There was silence at first on the other end of the phone, but then he spoke these words:

"Honey, I know several good men who at one time or another deserved prison but didn't get caught. In fact, I myself am just a sinner saved by grace. I could have gone to jail for some of the things I did when I was younger. I like Carl. I can see how much he loves you, and I know he will be a fine, strong husband."

As Christians, that's how all of us are supposed to respond when confronted by those who have failed miserably in life. But the truth is, we usually tend to fall into judgment or criticism and keep "those kind" at arm's length. I know, because I had been one of "those kind" for most of my life. So here was this man, Karen's father, a man who had been less than loving to her high-school boyfriends, now giving us his blessing. When I heard this, it helped explain why Karen took a chance on me in the first place. She had been nurtured in a home that practiced what they preached. She learned early on about God's grace and how none of us deserve it, yet it's still freely given. She learned that nothing can separate a person from the love of God and that the greatest miracle he performs is rescuing people from themselves—turning the mess they've made of their lives into something beautiful for the sake of his kingdom.

Who *wouldn't* want to marry someone like that?

Carl at age six, 1952   **Carl at age 13, 1959**

**Carl with his brother and sister,
Phil and Norma, around 1958**

Vietnam 1969/ 1970

**Serving in Vietnam
around 1969 /1970**

**Army drill sergeant,
1971/ 1972**

**Youngest drill sergeant
in the battalion**

Tennessee State Prison, 1979

**Engaged! Summer of 1980
"She was the most beautiful
thing I'd ever seen."**

Karen Brown becomes Mrs. Carlson.
November 26, 1980

With our first son, Joshua, on the beach in 1983

A family now, 1983

Carl and Josh, age 6, 1987

With our second son, Philip, 1987

**Our third son, Michael,
at 18 months, in 1994**

**Our fourth son, Stephen,
at three months, in 1994**

All four boys, 1996

Family vacation at Estes Park, Colorado, August 2008

With Stephen, Philip, and Michael, November 2008

Philip working with some of our Men of Valor children.

Deep Sea fishing with my four sons and their friend, Chad Guerra, in St. Augustine, Florida, June 2010

Josh is 29! October, 2010

Our boys at the Lake House, June 2011

Celebrating Philip's Birthday, September 2011

A typical Sunday afternoon following church

Family reunion in the mountains, Thanksgiving 2011

Now we have a daughter.
Josh's wife, Janna, has joined the
family! Married Sept. 18, 2012

Celebrating Josh's birthday, October 2012

Michael completes Marine Boot Camp. June 14, 2013

What a catch!
Michael, home on leave, fishing with
Dad and Stephen, June 2013

34 years together in 2014
I love her now more than ever.

Stephen completes Marine Boot Camp. April 9, 2014

Michael and Stephen, American Patriots. Semper Fi!
April 12, 2014

A Day on the Lake with Philip, September 2014

Fishing Getaway with my two oldest boys, September 2014

I am grateful for this calling.

The Men of Valor Jericho Project
Some of God's mightiest future warriors are
currently behind prison walls. The Lord will be
found when we seek him with all our hearts. He
is the God of redemption, reconciliation, and
hope. He's in the business of changing lives.

The Men of Valor Staff, dear friends and fellow warriors.
Not pictured: Dale Still, Marlo Wilt and Karen Carlson

A rendering of our vision for the M.O.V. complex

Perfect example of grace

As it turned out, Karen's dad became ill by the fall of that same year and was unable to attend our wedding. He died the next year at age forty-six, but he will always be a giant in my eyes. He gave Karen the gift every Christian daughter desires from her father—he favored her with his blessing. And he gave me the perfect example of grace. We couldn't have been more different, yet he somehow saw something in me that he accepted as good. I honestly can't take credit for that. He was a man of insight and he saw how serious I was about loving his daughter and serving God.

The months before we got married were the greatest months of my life. We weren't married and, of course, had no children, no serious responsibilities. During our senior year we had to make time to be together between classes and studying, but after graduation we were with each other constantly. It was a wonderful way to start a life together. I made parole and was allowed to leave the half-way house to move in with a buddy of mine. We lived in an apartment building that had a swimming pool. Every weekend we would hang out by the pool and grill chicken or steaks. It felt like a never-ending vacation. On Sunday we'd attend church together, then spend the rest of the day reading or picnicking, watching football on TV, or taking walks. While there are no guarantees when it comes to marriage, I believe that summer of spending so much time together gave us a foundation that would help us face the struggles that lay ahead. If we had begun to annoy each other we might have wondered if things wouldn't work out for a lifetime. But that wasn't the case. By the time our wedding day rolled around, we were eager to get going on a lifetime commitment.

Finding a job when you've got a record

Because I had benefitted so much from being given a second chance, I decided early on that I would work with kids who had backgrounds like mine: "throw-away kids"— youngsters without hope. I also knew that every job application had that impossible question: "Have you ever been convicted of a felony?" The new values given to me by my faith prohibited me from lying. It wouldn't have mattered anyway. They always do a background check, and if you lie you most certainly do not get the job.

Thankfully, two men decided to give me a chance— Ken Leary and Chet Leone. They believed in me and knew I was sincere about serving the Lord, so they arranged for Karen and me to serve as houseparents at the Nashville Group Home, a residential setting for boys who had been committed to the Department of Corrections. Can you imagine going from a summer where it was just Karen and me to suddenly becoming Mom and Dad to a houseful of boys who'd gotten into trouble with the law? I thought back to my own time in reform school and was determined to show these boys something I never had as a youngster: acceptance and love. I was 34. And Karen, at age 24, became the mother many of those boys had never had. She came well-equipped. When she was a student she had volunteered with a campus organization called Christian Workers Association (CWA) which, in part, ministered to young men residing at the local juvenile detention facility. You might call that a coincidence, but I call it God's preparing her.

One of the many reasons I loved that job was it gave me the flexibility to enroll at Tennessee State University to begin working on my Master's Degree. I wanted to be as trained and educated as possible to do my best in serving these kids. God had called me to work with troubled people, and I knew that an advanced degree would open up more possibilities for that. For the next three years Karen and I poured ourselves into the lives of the kids in the group home while I attended classes. Nothing is more rewarding than seeing a rebellious, angry young man lose the chip on his shoulder and turn his life around. We thoroughly enjoyed our time there. I eventually earned my Master's in Guidance and Counseling. Once I did, I was given an opportunity to work for the government. Which turned out to be an eye-opening experience in inefficiency and bureaucracy.

A crash course in how government programs work

The program—Jobs for Tennessee Graduates, or JTG—looked good on paper. The goal was for us to go into public high schools and work with a special curriculum to teach high school seniors job attainment and retention skills. The incentive for kids to sign up for this program was the promise of a decent job that carried the possibility of upward mobility. That's where the program broke down. All the program was really designed to do was to get a kid a job—any job. We promised these youngsters we'd place them in a decent job if they completed the program but then sent them to flip burgers at McDonald's or slop soapy rags at the car wash. In other words, we were lying to them. When they signed up, *we* were the ones with the nice jobs. Through the grace of God and my own grit and determination, I was able to place a handful of kids into meaningful work where they actually had a chance to turn it into a career. But overall, the program wasn't working. It was another waste of taxpayers' money. I'm sure it had been initially designed with the best intentions. I read somewhere that whatever the government can do, the private sector can do better. This job confirmed that.

Working with these high school students also gave me an education on the public school system in Nashville. In one of our first lessons, I handed out sample job applications and gave them their assignment: "This is the first thing you get when you apply for a job.

So take the next few minutes to fill it out and then we'll go over it together."

I figured once they were finished I would go through each item on the application, give them tips that might give them an advantage over other applicants, and answer questions. About half the kids just sat there staring at the application. That seemed odd. Were they being belligerent? After fifteen minutes, I announced that it was time to turn in their applications and was greeted by loud protests.

"I'm not finished!"

"Hey, don't rush me!"

"Can't we have more time?"

These kids were all seniors. They would soon be graduating, receiving a diploma that presumably indicated they had received a decent education. But half the students could not read at a sixth-grade level, and most of them had difficulty writing a complete sentence. Fifteen minutes should have been plenty of time to fill out a simple job application, but it wasn't, and I was shocked. Forget the job skills—these kids would go nowhere if they couldn't read. So I spent an inordinate amount of time and energy just trying to teach these seniors how to read and write.

After twelve years in the city's public school system, these students didn't stand a chance. I realize it's not entirely our schools' fault. There were dedicated teachers in the school district, but they seldom got the support they needed to do their jobs well. Students who struggled were passed on to the next level instead of being given remedial help, which only put them further behind. Most of the "at risk" kids came from tough home situations and likely didn't have a mom or dad read to them when they were young. Neither had I. Unfortunately, I don't have answers to the public education crisis, but something's wrong if students make it to their senior year in high school without being able to read.

I hung on for three years, trying to be part of the solution and not simply complain. But I reached the point where it was clear we weren't making progress. I was letting those kids down because we had lied to them about the kinds of jobs we could get for them. Why should they sign up for this "innovative" extra-curricular program if they ended up scooping french fries next to a buddy who had never participated in the program?

At the end of my third year with JTG, I told my supervisor I was leaving.

As a matter of principle, it was the right thing to do. But in the real world we lived in, it was risky. We already had our first son, Joshua, and by then we had welcomed our second son, Philip. We were a young family with a mortgage, bills, and student loans. This was 1986, when the U.S. economy was slowing down, and I had no way of knowing that Black Monday—when the entire global economy nearly shut down—was just around the corner.

Yet here I was, out of work with no one knocking on my door with a job offer. The perfect time to put my faith in God to the test.

8

Jumping without a Parachute

Through my earlier work at the Metropolitan Juvenile Detention Center, I had met and become good friends with a man named Ed Hunley, Chaplain of the detention center. He and I had stayed in touch after I left the Nashville Group Home to go to work for the government. One day toward the end of my time with JTG, I mentioned my disillusionment with the government-run program. That's when he gave me a kick in the butt.

"You need to start your own non-profit ministry working directly with kids to keep them out of trouble."

I'd never thought of doing anything like that and wasn't sure where to start. But I thought a good place to begin was with Karen. Here she was a young mother, and her husband had quit his job—their only source of income. We did not have extra money laying around to live on while I tried to figure out what I was going to do. I had a responsibility to take care of our little family, but I also felt this might be a God thing—that Ed was the messenger relaying God's call to do something that seemed almost impossible.

I came home from work one night, worn out from dealing with the bureaucracy and futility of a government job. After dinner, I brightened up because this was my favorite part of the day: spending time with Karen and our boys. Whether it was kicking a soccer ball around in the back yard or wrestling with them on the living room floor, we treasured this time together as a family.

Karen and I also cherished the time the two of us had together alone after putting the kids to bed. We'd been married for a little over five years. Being married isn't a cakewalk, and we had our struggles like any married couple. But we managed to face every difficulty together, and that strengthened our relationship. On this particular night, though, I was about to spring something on her that would take us into uncharted territory.

Karen knew about my frustration working for JTG. I had talked often about looking for another job, so when I told her I wanted to talk about the future, she probably thought I was going to seek her input on a new job I'd been offered. Which was exactly what I planned to do. Only this "job" didn't pay anything.

We sat on the couch as we often did, as I explained that I thought God was calling me to start my own ministry—an outreach to young kids to keep them out of trouble. I laid it all out for her—how I hadn't figured yet exactly what this ministry would look like, what it would specifically do, where it would operate, or where I would get the money to run it. In other words, as I told Karen, "I'm starting a new work, but for now I have no idea where the money's coming from."

She didn't remind me that we had a mortgage and that if we missed a payment we could lose our home. She didn't mention that we could lose our health insurance. The word "money" didn't come up at all. She refrained from telling me what we both knew: I had no experience leading *anything*.

Instead, she listened to my speech and then replied, "What a great idea!"

Which really didn't surprise me. Karen has a heart for the Lord, and if she believes God is behind something, she is not going to stand in the way. She had this trust that God will always provide for those who obey and serve him, which was a blessing because we were about to put that simple trust to the test.

To be perfectly honest, Karen's approach to this step of faith gave *me* encouragement. She told me how countless times as a child she watched her parents endure hardships and how no matter how discouraged they became, they didn't give up. As she told me, "Whenever they placed their trust in Jesus, he never left them stranded. And he won't abandon us either."

My "pass-the-cap" budget

With nothing but a dream, we started what eventually became known as the YMCA Community Action Project, or YCAP. At the beginning, we didn't have a name. It was just Karen and me and an old New York Yankees baseball cap. No board of directors and no support system in place. No office. No money. Nothing. I recruited about seven to eight guys who believed in me, and we met at the old juvenile detention center.

I explained what my dream was to these men: a ministry to work with high at-risk kids involved in the juvenile criminal system. After explaining that I had no start-up money, then answering questions, I took off my old baseball cap and literally passed it around. That was my income. And that's how we lived for the first few months of YCAP. It wasn't much, but we were grateful for every penny. We never missed a mortgage payment or a meal. There's a verse in the Bible that says, "Trust in the Lord with all your heart and lean not on your own understanding," and that describes what we were doing. The only thing I understood was that those kids in the detention center needed God, and we would do our best to show them his love.

When we started YCAP, we didn't have long range goals. As far as I was concerned, I could spend the rest of my life coming alongside kids like these and helping them get their lives on track. It wasn't long before I discovered what I basically knew all along from my own experience. These kids had little to no support at home. Most came from poor families. The majority had no fathers in their lives; their moms did their best but often lacked basic parenting skills. In other words, we could do a lot of good for these kids while they were locked up, but they returned to an environment which drew them back into the things that got them locked up in the first place. If we wanted to make a genuine difference, we had to not only minister to the kids but reach out to their families as well.

We expanded our work to include services for the families. Again, it was pretty basic stuff—visiting homes, making sure they had food, encouraging them, praying with them. Word spread, and our ministry started to grow. Various people began to support us financially; I'm convinced now that they were sent by God. It also gained the attention of a guy named James (J) Lawrence, who worked with the local YMCA. J was one of the original eight men who had initially supported me. He was so impressed with what we were doing that he obtained a grant for us to continue meeting the needs of the community, which is how we got our name. After a number of months of passing the baseball cap, we were now a fully registered non-profit organization. I convinced a small group of men to serve on our first board of directors, and we were off and running. A few years later we joined the YMCA, an organization that has historically reached out to disadvantaged people.

The challenges of managing growth

And things began to get rolling. Our little ministry expanded as other organizations began referring people to us. What started with just Karen and me and a few good men grew into an organization that employed sixteen full-time, dedicated workers who went out into the community with only one goal: to help troubled kids and their families. We were blessed with many others who saw what we were doing and reached out generously. Multitudes of volunteers signed up to help.

Karen and I attended First Church of the Nazarene in Nashville. As our ministry grew, our pastor, Dr. Millard Reed, gave us a house the church owned. On a handshake! He knew we needed a group home for boys and handed us the keys to the place. No contract. No restrictions. Amazing. The house sat directly across the street from the church.

Pastor Reed believed in what we were doing. I have to think he might have received a call or two from folks in the church who weren't pleased with having "those kind" so close to the church. If that happened, it didn't stop him from doing what he thought was right. We rolled up our sleeves and went to work re-modeling the house.

Many good folks from the church stepped up and helped with the remodeling; in particular, a man named

Don Knotts. But there were so many others. Our church's youth pastor, Doug Runyon, welcomed these kids into the youth group. This church was basically a middle to upper-middle class church, and mostly white, yet if you visited their youth meetings on any given Sunday you'd see all those youngsters from nice families sitting beside our kids of all races and colors, getting along and having a great time together.

Our primary emphasis with YCAP was spiritual growth, education, and relationship. Once a kid started lagging behind in class, he was a prime candidate for dropping out. And once he got out on the streets, our next contact with him was often in jail or some other lock up.

So, three times a week, as soon as school was out we'd send vans all over the city to pick up students for our after school program. Initially these were kids referred to us by the courts—kids who had been in trouble with the law. But as word spread about our program, we received calls from school principals and guidance counselors seeking our help.

Since we didn't have our own facilities, we had to find other organizations willing to share theirs, which is how I met Charlie Finchum. Charlie was the executive director of the Nashville Boys and Girls Club. When he learned about us, he offered the use of his building. It was perfect, with rooms for academic tutoring, counseling, and feeding the kids. It had a full gym, where the boys could play and let off steam. We dropped them off at the YMCA, First Nazarene Church, and other places around the city. Then the fun began. What do you do with about fifty kids spread out over several locations?

Our plan was simple. We had the boys for several hours after school before we took them home. So we started tutoring them—helping with their homework and making sure they were caught up in their classes. We got them up and moving with various athletics like soccer, basketball, or other sports that burn off energy. We'd feed them, knowing it's hard to concentrate on an empty stomach. Many of the kids took care of themselves at home, and this likely was the only nutritious meal they got all day. Mostly we'd just give them our time, showing them Jesus and his love for them. More than anything, kids desperately need to know they are loved and that someone is there for them.

Who were those *someones*? God blessed us with an amazing resource of volunteers: ordinary men and women who donated a couple hours of their time three days a week to work with the boys. In the early years we had a few women who had a great impact on the children: Ava Laws, Sara Chilton, Henrietta Hagler, and Mary Lee Fielder. Our volunteers were anything but ordinary. When ordinary people have free time they head for the golf course or the shopping mall. These men and women showed up with hearts full of love and a desire to help kids. We linked each of the kids up with a mentor, a big brother—men who appreciated the blessings they were given and wanted to give back. They gave the kids positive role models to look up to, which is a big deal. Often, the only adults they had to look up to in their neighborhoods were drug dealers and gang bangers.

One man in particular who the Lord sent us was John Grayken. John not only became a mentor to two brothers, he later came on the YCAP board and eventually became our board chairman. John was instrumental in the opening of our YCAP Group Home, and he was the driving force behind us joining the YMCA fully. He was also a significant financial supporter. John has been a tremendous blessing to both ministries—YCAP and Men of Valor— and a great blessing to me personally and to my family.

Now I know why they call it burnout

For eleven years I poured myself into YCAP. My title may have been Founder and Director, but if you asked my staff they would have said I was the CMM: chief micro manager. I had never led anything before and had always been a hands-on guy, so I tried to ride herd on everything that was going on. I was constantly recruiting volunteers, raising funds, helping out at the centers, and yes, hovering over the operation. I wrote the checks, did the bookkeeping, answered my own phone, and had a hard time saying no to anyone who needed some of my time. Twelve-hour days were the norm, and it wasn't unusual for me to be on the job from early morning to past midnight.

This ministry was running me instead of the other way around. It's one thing to be committed to a vision, but I had allowed mine to consume me. The joy which had sustained me for so long had evaporated.

I was burnt toast, but I didn't know what to do about it. I made the mistake of believing the ministry depended on me; that if I even took a vacation it would suffer. By this time I was thinking about more than just a vacation. There were days I felt like walking away. I had never been a quitter, but I was so overextended that quitting didn't seem so bad. Even as I considered leaving YCAP, I'd look at the great people on our staff and the hundreds of volunteers. What would they think if I just walked away? I'd be letting them down. To my way of thinking, the honorable thing to do would be to bury those distracting thoughts, maybe pray harder, and hope for the best. Yet deep inside I knew. I couldn't keep hanging on. And by the way, during this time, Karen and I added two more sons to our family: Michael and Stephen.

Something had to change.

9

Recalibrating

I had never heard the term "burnout" other than when I put the pedal to the metal in one of my fancy cars from my wilder days. But that was what I was experiencing. I had my foot on the accelerator the whole time I was leading YCAP. I didn't know any other way to get things done since that's what it took to turn vision into reality. Unfortunately, I didn't know a better way to lead once our ministry got up and running. As I gradually came to the end of my rope, my colleagues bore the brunt of my frustrations. Which is why my departure was not exactly resisted when I finally waved the white flag of surrender. Some of my people were relieved to see me go. The lessons I had learned, the mistakes I had made, had affected and impacted them too.

I was spent. My spiritual tank was on empty. I was walking in the flesh, flying by the seat of my pants. I made decisions that I regret to this day. But God, who is rich in mercy, used my failures to drive me to him. I began to seek him in a deeper fashion, spending time searching, praying, and crying out for guidance. I surrounded myself with Godly men who would hold me accountable.

God used these experiences, and my brokenness, to lead me into a deeper walk with him. He was preparing me to later launch Men of Valor and the Jericho Project, learning to submit my ways to his. As it is in many cases, God's way up . . . was down.

Normally when something like this happens, the next step is to start looking for another job. We still had that mortgage and now *four* kids to feed, so I assumed I'd take a short break, then pound the pavement. But I discovered how caring and compassionate the people of that YMCA were; in particular, the YCAP Board of Directors. They offered me a sabbatical and to continue paying me during that time. They could have simply cut me off, but they didn't, and I'll be forever grateful to them for their compassion and generosity; especially Larry Baker, Henry McFadden, Tony Giarratana, the YCAP board members, and Clark Baker, CEO of the Metro YMCA.

Seeking God's fresh touch

Having never experienced a sabbatical, I wasn't sure what to do with myself, but I knew the term came from the word Sabbath. I needed rest and a fresh touch from

God. I awoke early each morning and went to a nearby park. I had a thermos of coffee, a bottle of water, my Bible, and several books written by "giants" of the faith: Max Lucado, Charles Swindoll, John MacArthur, Charles Stanley. I immersed myself in the things of God. I had wandered away from him by relying on my own strength rather than his. I would return to that place of living fully within his will.

As I read, I also prayed, listening for God to say something because I sure didn't have much to say. I'd usually end up crying. I was so broken that it would overwhelm me at times. On many occasions, Ken Leary would join me. Ken was one of the first men to believe in me those many years earlier, and he wasn't giving up on me. He would listen to my confusion and pain and reassure me that God still loved me and wanted me to serve him. He prayed over me, and I felt I was in the presence of a saint as he lifted me up to the Lord.

The days stretched into weeks and the weeks into months, but I returned to the park daily, seeking God. I needed direction. There were times when God seemed close, but other times when I felt he was done with me.

Heading back to prison

Back when I was a student at Trevecca, I worked part time on the loading docks of a trucking company. To do so, I was required to join the Teamster's Union. I still had my union card, so I considered returning to the docks, finding a job loading trailers, and forgetting this business of ministry. The YMCA wouldn't keep paying me forever, and by getting a job on the docks I'd be able to care for my family. I had begun doubting that I was cut out for ministry. Maybe YCAP had been a mistake. Why would God give me another chance to screw something up? Every now and then I'd hear those voices from my childhood: "You'll never amount to much," and "We don't want your kind around here."

This was more than burnout. This was a struggle for my soul.

During my sabbatical, I visited a former kid from YCAP who'd since gotten into serious trouble and was now locked up in prison. I never wanted to see the inside of a prison again, but I'd become fond of that kid while he was in YCAP. So every week I'd visit him, wanting to encourage him. I knew something about his rough family life, and I hated for him to fall back into the cycle of crime that traps so many in urban America. I remembered well what it was like to be in prison myself with no support from the outside.

One day I went to visit him and discovered he'd been transferred to a different prison. As I turned to leave, another inmate walked up to me.

"Can I talk to you?" he asked.

"Sure, you can talk to me," I answered, and motioned to one of the conference rooms.

We were total strangers, but he began telling me his story: just like that, out of the blue; not only his history, but how he felt as a man. He was ashamed of the way he'd let his mom down. He missed seeing see his kids. He worried about what he was going to do when he got out. He knew how hard it was to make something of your life once you had a criminal record. I encouraged him the best I could and prayed with him, then left.

The next week I went back to check on him and yet another guy approached me, asking if we could talk. Once again, I listened. I could sense how much this time apart meant to him. I recalled having only one visit from my brother the entire time I was locked up. As I left that second time, I couldn't shake the impression that these men had approached me for a reason. Perhaps something bigger was going on. Maybe the Lord was using *them* to talk to me. Wouldn't that be just like God? Here I was lost and floundering in a spiritual desert, seeking his voice, and he used a couple of inmates to open my eyes.

While seeking his will for my next move, I formed two small groups for the express purpose of receiving counsel concerning the future. "Without counsel, purposes are disappointed, but in the multitude of counselors they are established." (Proverbs 15:22) The groups met twice each, and they did not communicate with each other. When their meetings were concluded,

I met with them. Both groups were unanimous in their recommendations: I needed to start a prison ministry.

It was never my plan to go back into prison. Any prison. I hated prisons. I had visited that young man because he was one of my YCAP kids. Yet it was evident the Lord was working on me. No huge revelations, only a clear understanding that God was leading me to serve him by reaching out to men in prison. If I had learned anything over the years, it's that if God is calling you, you'd best obey. Remember Jonah?

A mess of misfits

Eventually I got in touch with the two men who had been with me from the beginning, Ken Leary and Chet Leone. I shared with them what was going on and how I knew God was leading me to start another ministry— this time going into prisons and working with inmates. I understood first-hand how difficult it is for men to make it after serving their time, and I felt I could help prepare them to be successful outside of prison. Chet and Ken encouraged me to go for it. I contacted some other men who had helped me at YCAP and asked if they would help me get this work off the ground: John Grayken, Louie Buntin, Phil Hickey, Tony Giarratana, Bill Lee, Jim Denton, Jack Blier, Larry Baker, David Pitzer, Rolus Smith, Jerry Breast, Adam Hicks, Brian Reyes, Jeff Sexton, Jimmy Webb, and J.D. Elliott- plus, of course, Ken and Chet. Each of these men played a significant role in helping me turn my next dream into a reality. They were completely used by God to make it come together. Without these men, and others, there would not be a Men of Valor. They supported, encouraged, and kept MOV on solid financial footing. Their financial support and encouragement has truly helped sustain Men of Valor to this day.

We named our ministry Men of Valor based on the story of when David selected a crew of misfits to join his army. They later became known as David's Mighty Men of Valor. I knew first-hand what God can do with a guy in trouble. If God could do something good with my life, I could be part of a bigger plan to do the same for others. One thing was certain: I'd have plenty of opportunities. Between 1980 and today (2014), the prison population in America has increased by 500 percent. More than two million people are locked up. The United States makes up five percent of the world's population, but we incarcerate twenty-five percent of the world's prisoners—the highest incarceration rate in the world. Two-thirds of prisoners who are released are re-arrested within three years. That makes me one of the lucky ones. But this was anything but luck. It was God's grace. I wanted to see other men like me experience the same thing and turn their lives around to become productive citizens, contributing to society.

I also had a burden for the families of these men. There are nearly two million children in this country who have one or both parents in prison. The average age of a child with a parent in prison is eight. Twenty-two percent of these children are under the age of five. These are the forgotten innocent victims of crime, and more than seventy-percent of them are going to end up in prison themselves unless effective intervention occurs.

Typically, what happens is that Dad gets carted off to prison, leaving Mom to put food on the table and take care of the kids. It's just too much. This isn't criticism of single moms, but the reality of how difficult it is for one parent to do the job of two. Throw poverty into the mix, and hopelessness, even despair, can set in, and it's almost impossible to make any progress.

As the child approaches his teenage years he starts running with the wrong crowd. It could be a gang or just a bunch of lost children, but either way, they show him how to swipe stuff off the shelves at stores, how to smash a car window and grab a camera left on the seat, or how to sell a little weed. It isn't long before these petty crimes turn into something more serious, then eventually, they get caught. They always do. I wanted to be the effective intervention that helped reduce the chance of this happening.

The plan for MOV was to go into Nashville's prisons to work with men who were getting close to their release dates. This is when they would be most receptive to help. Once this was established, we would develop a program for their families. On paper it looked good, and I began to get excited again. I recalled reading about Ezekiel in the Bible and how he was in a valley with skeletons scattered around the ground—dry bones, he called them. God breathed life into those old bones, and they got up and became "a vast army." The skeletons represented the people of Israel, but they could have represented me and the guys Men of Valor would be training. I had been as dead as those old dry bones as I prayed on that park bench every day. Then God breathed his life into me. He restored my soul by calling me to serve him again. I would now have the opportunity to let that same breath of God restore the lives of other men who had been ignored by society.

I had no idea what God had in store, but I was ready to find out.

10

Breaking Down the Walls

"All dressed up and nowhere to go." That was me: fired up with a new ministry—a board, an office, but not much to do. Yet.

At first, I simply continued visiting inmates and holding Bible studies inside the prison. Every now and then I took some volunteers with me. Over time, as we began to grow, and with the Lord's blessing, I was able to hire a couple of men to help me create a program that would work. We needed permission from the prison officials to expand our efforts. We needed a formal process for equipping men for success after their release. To expand the program, though, we needed money to pay for staff, for materials, for rent, for utility bills, etc.

One major change in the field of corrections over previous years was that private companies had formed partnerships with various state governments to handle all aspects of running prisons. Based on my earlier negative experience in working for the government, I felt this was a step in the right direction. To keep their contracts with the government, these companies had to do a superior job and for less money. They had to earn the right to keep their jobs. This usually brings out the best in a company.

A very important "cold call"

After a number of years working with the men at Charles Bass Correctional Facility, I became aware of Prison Fellowship's IFI program: Inner-Change Freedom Initiative. The program was highly structured, working all day with the men in their program using both staff and volunteers, and required one year for each inmate. A couple of MOV board members and I flew to Iowa to look into it, and we were impressed. I sent Curt Campbell to check out a second IFI program, this time in Texas, and he returned enthusiastic. I went to my board of directors and explained to them that we had found the direction MOV needed to go

We drew up a plan and presented it to the Commissioner of the Tennessee Department of Corrections. He turned us down flat, thanks to the so called "establishment clause" separating church and state. The evil one has used that clause more than once to keep faith based ministries out of the prisons.

One of our many volunteers at MOV, a young man by the name of Will Trapp, called me one day and told me I needed to meet with his father-in-law, John Ferguson, President and CEO of CCA—Corrections Corporation of America. CCA operates more than sixty prisons in sixteen states. This was the big time, and John was the head man. We scheduled a meeting, and four of my MOV board members went with me. I'm sure John had bigger fish to fry that day, but he graciously listened as I laid out my vision for helping a tiny percentage of the 80,000 prisoners his company had incarcerated across the nation. He never flinched when I told him the mission of Men of Valor: to win men in prison to Jesus Christ and disciple them.

To say that John Ferguson, CEO of CCA, was instrumental to the success of Men of Valor and the launching of the Jericho Project would be like saying air is instrumental to our ability to breathe. He not only allowed us into the prison but gave it his personal stamp of approval. Recently John has moved on to become Chairman of the CCA board. John's successor, Damon Hininger, the current CEO and President of CCA, has followed in John's footsteps and been totally supportive of Men of Valor also. Both these men were sent by God to help us in this work.

With the help of many men who stepped up financially, in particular Cal Turner, we launched what we call The Jericho Project. With Cal's solid financial backing, we were able to hire enough staff to run the program. God sent John and Cal and other men to make this a reality.

John Ferguson then did something that was unprecedented: he gave us an entire housing unit inside the prison! He provided office space for three full-time and two part-time MOV staff. This is where they would work every day, in offices fully equipped with computers, phones, file cabinets, and desks. The men we counsel all reside in this one large housing unit, where they spend nine hours a day engaged in a rigorous, highly structured program. The Jericho Project is an intensive twelve-month biblically-based curriculum designed to teach men purpose and equip them for success upon their release from prison. In the Bible, Jericho was a city held captive by God's enemies, but by obeying God, Joshua took back the city as "the walls came tumbling down." We wanted to break down the walls that held these men captive: the hate, the drug/alcohol addictions, the anger and rage, the abuse, and so many other issues.

I've never been to seminary, but I've been told by those who have that our Jericho Project curriculum is nearly the equivalent of a seminary education. It has also been suggested that *every* Christian should experience this level of "life instruction." We help these men put their lives back together, addressing the reasons that got them headed down the wrong path in the first place, and giving them practical skills so when they get out they will have something to offer an employer.

The Jericho Project curriculum is divided into four phases, each lasting three months. At any given time, we have between forty-five to fifty men enrolled in the program. These are men who will be released within a year to eighteen months and have demonstrated that they are serious about improving their lives. They need to be completely dedicated because the program we put them through is tough. Men of Valor staff and volunteers work with these men for twelve months, five days a week, approximately nine hours a day. It's intensive because they have to undo a lifetime of wrong thinking. Rebuilding lives takes time.

How do you rebuild a man?

A typical day in The Jericho Project starts with devotions at 7:30 in the morning, developing the practice of beginning a man's day with God. We hope they will carry this habit with them into their outside lives. We're not just building good men, but godly men—committed to loving and serving God and less likely to return to their old ways. The Bible tells us that "if anyone is in Christ, he is a new creation," which is why it is crucial to lead these men into a personal relationship with Jesus. While there are no guarantees in life, developing and maintaining a close relationship with Jesus helps keep all of us from going astray. Everything we do with these men begins with a biblical perspective.

They all suffer from poor self-esteem, so one of the classes in the curriculum is called "Son of the King." Their value as a person doesn't come from being good or doing the right thing, but from the fact that they are true sons of God; that God created them in his own image and for a unique purpose. Like me, these guys have been told numerous times that they're worthless, will never change, and that no one wants them around. That message is hard to overcome, but once you learn you belong to the King of kings, you can begin to understand your true worth.

We're not afraid to tell these men about sin and its power to keep them enslaved. In a course called "Bondage Breakers," we teach that sin is the core issue which put them in the mess they're in. In some circles—even religious ones—it's not popular to talk about sin and Satan, but no one can live a victorious life without acknowledging there is an evil force seeking to deceive and destroy. The Bible warns that all Christians will struggle against the world, the flesh, and the devil. We are all vulnerable. We teach our men the reality of sin and give them powerful truths that will help them break their stubborn habits or private sins.

In addition to the Bible, which is the core textbook for The Jericho Project curriculum, we assign other Christian books to inform and inspire these men to live up to the potential God has for them: books like *The Purpose-Driven Life* by Rick Warren, *Wild at Heart* by John Eldridge, *In the Grip of Grace* by Max Lucado, and one of my favorites, *The Ragamuffin Gospel* by Brennan Manning. Our men are "ragamuffins"—beating themselves up for their failures and viewing God as a stern disciplinarian keeping track of all their sins. When they fully understand grace—that God loves them no matter what they've done—real change can happen in their lives. This is something I have personally not been able to fully comprehend: God's grace. I have experienced it by virtue of my life but have not fully understood it.

We must do more than just work on the spiritual lives of these men, so The Jericho Project covers a lot of practical territory, as well. Many men in prison had a drug or alcohol problem on the outside and will, from day one upon release, have easy access to both. Their old friends will be more than willing to help them score some weed or cocaine or anything else. Just one quick stop at the corner liquor store is all it takes to send them spiraling down into the valley of addiction again. We bring people in from Narcotics Anonymous and Alcoholics Anonymous to help them learn how to stay clean.

Even with good intentions, once the men are released they're going to face enormous hurdles, so we put them through a three-month course dealing with specific obstacles: reconciling with family, hard work for low pay, rejection, etc. Most people on the outside don't want anything to do with an ex-con. And with today's technology and laws, you can see exactly where every ex-con is living in your community. Even if a guy has done his time and paid for his crime, it follows him the rest of his life.

Our mentors: key to success

As crucial as all these lessons are, the real genius of The Jericho Project is the mentoring that goes with it. The entire time a man is in the program, he is assigned a free-world mentor, who meets with him one-on-one every week. If a man finishes The Jericho Project but still has a few months to go before his release, we don't forget about him. He continues receiving personal encouragement and accountability from his mentor. This helps explain why the Men of Valor programming results in a recidivism rate of less than fifteen percent, compared to the national average of seventy percent. Not only do our men receive great biblical and practical teaching through the curriculum, they each have a friend in their corner who takes the time to go into prison and meet with them.

Where do we find our mentors? From all walks of life—businessmen, lawyers, teachers, retirees, entrepreneurs, etc. The common denominator is that they love God and have a desire to share this love with others. One of our mentors is a gentleman named David Floyd, a senior citizen who signed on to mentor a guy I'll refer to as A.C. Even after A.C. was released from prison, David continued mentoring him. These two men are about as different as you can be: one is white, the other black. One is in his seventies, the other is in his forties. One has lived a squeaky clean life, the other served time in prison. But if you saw them together, you'd see they are best friends. That's what the love of God can do.

"David Floyd is my guy," A.C. told me. "He came in and took my hand and modeled for me what it is like to walk the Christian walk. To have a guy like David come inside and mentor me in prison and then continue to walk with me after I was out is truly a sign that God is with me."

This scene is repeated over and over again—fifty to sixty times a year—as we regularly start up new groups of men in the program. As each man is released from prison, the mentoring continues.

According to Curt Campbell, who heads up our Jericho Project, "It's great to see a man find God through our program and be mentored during the remainder of his incarceration. But if it stops there, the deck is so stacked against him that he's going to have a hugely difficult time making it on the outside."

A few weeks ago I received a copy of a letter that one of our Jericho Project men wrote to a volunteer in the program. It sums up better than I could just what this program does for men whom the rest of society has given up on:

It has been two years since I saw my little girl due to my choices and actions. Feeling lost and void, I got information about the Men of Valor "Jericho Project." I asked to be interviewed for it and was brought into the ministry. I knew of Jesus but did not know him personally. I now see that Men of Valor was God's lifeline to me. As crazy as it sounds, this has been one of the best years of my life, for I have come to know, love, and trust Jesus Christ with all aspects of my life. Jesus has now filled the void I have carried since I was a teen, dead set on doing things my way. I thank him every day for great Christian examples such as you men who believe in the power of Christ to change a man's life. I can and will strive to be the best possible man he wills me to be.

I am immensely proud of the staff and volunteers who give so much of themselves to The Jericho Project day in and day out. In October 2013, eleven men in Jericho came to the Lord and were baptized. Our greatest need is mentors, both for the men and for their wives and children in our family/children's ministry.

But that's just the beginning.

What happens when these men are released from prison?

11

Re-entering Society

It's 5:45 in the morning—the slowly climbing sun casts a faint glow over the hills east of Nashville, bringing with it the promise of another warm day. The birds have just begun their morning choruses to accompany the wake-up call that rings through the building where seven men have been sleeping soundly. Jerome wants to roll over for another few winks but he knows better. He's got a little over an hour to make his bed, tidy up his bunk area, hit the weight room, shower, grab some breakfast, and make his sack lunch. And if he's learned anything in his two weeks here, it's that showing up late for *anything* is unacceptable.

Welcome to Couchville.

If you drive by CCA—the prison where we run our Jericho Project—there's a good chance you'll see a guy walking out the gate carrying a white bag. In that white bag are his earthly possessions. He is leaving. He is a free man. The fact that he's walking tells you one thing: he doesn't have anyone in his life who cares about him enough to drive over and give him a ride. These are the guys who will be back before too long. I know exactly where they're going—back to their same old friends to do the same old things that got them into trouble in the first place. Even the way they walk tells you they know their chances of making it are somewhere between slim and none.

Could you live without hope?

The whole purpose of Men of Valor is hope—hope for men who have been disenfranchised. The Jericho Project begins the process, but these men need our continuing help in order to make a successful transition from being locked up to being free. Over ninety percent of these men come out of poverty, which only compounds the problems they face on the outside. One of their old friends might let them sleep on a couch as they go through the futile effort of finding a job. They have few marketable skills, but even if they were master craftsmen, their criminal record will usually close any doors that might have been opened slightly for them.

Many of these men have wives or girlfriends and children, but moving back in and trying to assume new responsibilities as husband and father brings a whole new set of problems. If they're one of the fortunate ones, they are welcomed back enthusiastically. But without counseling and other assistance, the marriage quickly falters. In most cases, they aren't welcomed back at all, which adds to the sense of hopelessness in these men.

Knowing these things, I wondered, "What if we could build our own aftercare campus, complete with houses for men, houses for families, and a multi-purpose building with a full gym? Man! Now that would be something." It would be a place away from the distractions of the city where men who successfully complete The Jericho Project can live for a while after their release from prison. We could do even more intensive work with families. I prayed about this dream and left it in the Lord's hands. I then went to the MOV Board of Directors with this new vision, and after much dialogue, we made the decision to move forward. We began our capital campaign (which is still going on today) and raised some money. This is how "Couchville" came about. A beautiful piece of property on Couchville Pike—just outside of Nashville— became available, complete with a large house that we could renovate into a home for eight men. It was perfect for our needs, so with a down payment and high hopes, we bought the property.

Many men have stepped up and helped with this undertaking: Jack Hooper, Louie Buntin, J.D. Elliott, Bill Freeman, Jimmy Webb, Eddie Hutton, Runcie Clements, Ben Sensing, John Ferguson, Steve Groom,

Rick and Andrea Carlton, Brett Beavers, Bill Lee, Jeff Dobyns, David Watts, Overton Thompson, Matt Cowan, Frank Burkholder, Paul Rutledge, Larry Kloess, John Avery, Gregg Turner, and Charles Irby, among others. We have a long way to go, but we are making steady progress.

Couchville, then, is the first phase of our Aftercare/Re-entry Program at Men of Valor. Raul Lopez runs this program, which is aimed at ensuring the men make a successful transition into society. Just like The Jericho Project, Couchville is highly structured with a distinct focus on helping these men grow as true men of God. But getting into Couchville is tough. Consider these requirements:

- The candidate must be *unanimously* recommended by The Jericho Project staff
- The candidate must demonstrate that he is *fully committed* to the program and will participate in *every* activity
- No personal vehicles are permitted at Couchville—we provide all necessary transportation
- No cell phones are allowed for any of the participants
- Random drug tests are performed
- No women are allowed on site
- No alcohol or drugs are allowed

If they violate any rules, they can be kicked out of the program. Because they are on parole, they must abide by the requirements set forth for them by their parole board and maintain regular meetings with their parole officer. These guys may be out of prison, but we keep them on a short leash.

For six months, the men at Couchville rise and shine at 5:45 each morning and hit the sack promptly at 10:00 p.m. By the time the lights are out, no one has trouble sleeping. In addition to an hour-long Bible study after breakfast, the men participate in regular Alcoholics Anonymous and Narcotics Anonymous meetings, "Manhood Training," and other planned activities. A volunteer organization called Victim Impact comes in once a week to help them understand how crime impacts victims—often by bringing in victims of crimes to share their ordeals. In addition to the teaching and training these men go through, they work about seven hours a day for a small business we created just to give them work experience and to put a few bucks in their pocket. EDS, or Everyday Dependable Services, is our small lawn-care business that provides a great service for consumers and a paycheck for the men. It's run by Tommy Mathis, who came to us with years of experience in the lawn care business. He does an incredible job with this business. In addition to giving the men a chance to earn a paycheck, EDS provides them with a sense of pride in their work. It may not seem like much to some people, but when you've been beaten down most of your life, seeing a freshly cut lawn and nicely trimmed landscape, which you did yourself, gives you a genuine sense of accomplishment.

It's not just hard work and no play. We're helping these men develop in all areas of their lives, so we have Friday Fun Nights, where they go bowling or to the movies or engage in other wholesome activities. This is to expose them to clean activities that can make them rounded as individuals. For the men who have families, we provide regular family visits to help them gradually re-enter family life. Because it is important to establish church attendance, we take them to local churches on Sunday mornings and Wednesday evenings. They have regular free time in the evenings to relax, read, or watch television in the community TV room. In short, we're introducing them to a lifestyle they may have never before experienced—one that is well-balanced and will keep them focused on the right things once they're completely on their own.

Every two weeks we have community service, where the men perform work in the community. This teaches them to "give back." All men who go to prison are takers; we want them to become givers instead.

Would you rent an apartment to an ex-con?

Once a man successfully completes his term at Couchville, we're not done with him. While Couchville does a great job building a strong foundation for these men, it's somewhat isolated from the real world. They're under our watchful eyes for awhile because we know how easily they can be tempted to fall back into old habits. The chances of them screwing up at Couchville aren't too high. But once they leave the friendly confines of this program, they must find a way to make it on their own. This can be tough. When he leaves prison, a man is given $35, a prison uniform without the number, and a bus ticket to anywhere in Tennessee. Because so many of them have burned their bridges with family, they typically end up on a sofa in someone's apartment—usually someone who's up to no good. With no job skills and a prison record, finding a job is about as easy as climbing Mt. Everest.

Knowing that all our good work at Couchville could go down the drain with one bad decision, we provide the men with transitional housing, another way God has blessed us through the generosity of others. Three businessmen who believe in what we do *gave* us ten apartments. Jimmy Webb, Kirby Davis, and Bill Freeman are successful Nashville businessmen who handed us the keys to these apartments so we can continue helping our men make a successful transition into society.

The idea behind the apartments is to provide safe, structured, and affordable housing designed to serve as a place of preparation for eventually moving out and getting a place of their own. In exchange for housing, each guy signs a contract which commits him to a variety of standards on how to live as a responsible citizen and godly man. We expect them to not only attend church regularly, but to find a church in which they can become involved and call their own. They are required to attend weekly Men of Valor Bible studies and other regularly scheduled meetings. To encourage them to give back to society, we require them, just as we do at Couchville, to participate in four hours of community service every other week. We conduct random drug testing and prohibit them from using alcohol. We're even fairly strict about the kinds of DVDs, magazines, and music they bring into the apartment—we refer to this as "keeping the ground holy."

To qualify for this program, the men must have jobs—something we help them with through various business contacts who have taken a leap of faith by agreeing to hire ex-convicts. A job is important for many reasons. To be successful once they are living independently, they will need to be employed—and stay employed. If they get fired or quit their job, they have to find a new one on their own in order to stay in the program. We also want them working so they will learn how to handle money wisely. Each apartment resident is responsible for paying all his utilities on time, to help him understand the importance of meeting his financial obligations. We require each resident to establish and maintain a budget that includes putting money into a savings account. The majority of these men come out of poverty. When you have nothing, things like budgeting and saving and paying your bills on time are irrelevant. We know from experience that when a man gets behind on his bills or runs out of money, he usually finds a way to get his hands on some money, and not always in a legitimate manner. When he learns how to handle his money, he will be less likely to revert to old habits. Finally, we are intent on helping these men avoid the things that can drag them back into their old ways.

If we don't help them, who will?

Some of these measures may seem extreme, but from my own experience I know they're necessary. Since the majority of society doesn't want to have anything to do with someone who's been to prison, ex-convicts are vulnerable to the vultures that exist in every community wanting to pull them back into the gutter. To the drug dealers and prostitutes, these guys are an easy source of income. To the thieves, they are partners who can help rob a liquor store. You and I don't have to worry much about those elements, but the men in our aftercare program would be sitting ducks without the structure and boundaries we place on them.

None of this aftercare would be possible if we didn't have people willing to take a chance on a guy with a rap sheet. Not many people are comfortable having former felons working in their backyards, but we have loyal customers keeping our E.D.S. lawn care guys busy. We have a number of local businesses who knowingly hire our men, often teaching them a new trade and providing ongoing employment after they complete the aftercare program.

And those apartments? I put that generous gift under the category of *miracle*. When a man leaves prison, he has no money and no job, which means nobody's going to rent him an apartment. He usually has to seek out one of his former friends for a place to live, which is the first step back into his old way of life. The remarkable thing about our transitional housing program is that since we opened it in 2003, we have had minimal problems, perhaps two or three incidents, which is amazing since there have been a couple of hundred men go through the program.

Our aftercare program disciples the men and gets them on their feet as men of God. We give them hope—a belief that they can be the kind of man God wants them to be. They have been beaten down by their choices and by the system, and our mission is to build them back up, helping them see they have value as children of God, created in his image. Nothing thrills my heart more than to witness this happen—to see them gain their dignity and strive to live lives pleasing to God.

Raul Lopez and his staff and volunteers do a tremendous job. One of our greatest challenges is helping the men find jobs. But we have lined up employers who will hire the men in our aftercare program, and they maintain contact with them after they graduate. It's like when a baby bird has tested its wings and is ready to leave the nest. We do everything we can to make sure these men will fly instead of fall. We prepare them to earn a living, manage their money, resist the temptations they will inevitably face, and continue to grow spiritually.

It takes time and the dedication of many volunteers to walk alongside a man, from his final months in prison to the point where he can live independently and successfully. This is the primary focus of Men of Valor. But what about his family? Who's helping them? For just about every man we work with, there are children and other loved ones who have to cope with his absence. It's a huge problem, and one I couldn't ignore.

12

The Forgotten Victims

Karen and I have been blessed with four wonderful sons. They are all grown now, but to me they'll always be my "boys." Although Karen deserves much of the credit for the way each of our sons has matured and developed, I was there for them as well. I coached Little League with our two oldest sons for a total of fifteen years, and basketball for all four of the boys for a total of nearly twenty years. I took them fishing, camping twice a year, and to many college and professional ballgames. We took family vacations each year, and we were Cub Scout den leaders. I endeavored through the years to teach my boys about God, with many conversations about what it is to be a real man. The Lord is still working on me, and my wife and sons know I am far from perfect, but I have done all I know how to be a good father. One thing I am absolutely sure of is that all four of my sons know how much I love them and how very proud I am of them. As I write this, our oldest son Joshua has a great position at Vanderbilt and is married to a beautiful Christian young woman, Janna, whom we love as a daughter. Philip is working hard in the air conditioning and heating business. Michael and Stephen, our youngest two, are United States Marines. Karen and I were both committed to our boys and endeavored to instill in them Christian values, but still, parenting wasn't always easy. Any way you slice it, being an effective, loving parent takes dedication that never, ever quits.

Now imagine what it must be like for a mother when the father of her children is in prison. Think of the child who is nine years old and sees her dad through a plexiglass window inside a strange and foreboding facility, after being patted down before going in. Consider the little boy sitting in his desk at school while someone makes fun of him because his daddy's in prison. Imagine Christmas with no tree, no stocking full of goodies, no presents brightly wrapped.

These are precious innocent children. It's not their fault that Dad's in prison, yet they have to pay the price. In most cases, these families had already struggled financially, but now that there's only one income— and not a big one—extreme poverty and all that it brings with it is the norm. If Mom works, it's usually at a minimum-wage job, so she can't afford child care. Youngsters left alone at home often end up running the streets and heading for trouble. Kids—especially boys—with a father in prison typically act out their anger and frustration, causing problems at school and at home. It's not Mom's fault—she's usually doing her best to earn a living and provide for her children. It's not the kids' fault when they act out or get in trouble—they lack the nurture and guidance they desperately need.

Breaking the cycle of poverty and crime

The welfare of children with a parent in prison is a huge and never-ending problem that contributes to the vicious cycle of poverty and crime. Nearly two million children in this country have a parent serving a sentence in prison—anywhere from 50-75,000 in Tennessee alone. Sixty-three percent of federal prisoners and fifty-five percent of state prisoners are parents of at least one child under eighteen. Seventy-five percent of the men we work with at Men of Valor are parents. The average age of children with an incarcerated parent is eight years old. Twenty-two percent are under the age of five.

Eighty-five percent of young men in prison grew up in fatherless homes. Ninety percent of homeless and runaway children are from fatherless homes. When all is said and done, seventy percent of these children will end up in prison unless some type of intervention occurs.

It doesn't make sense to help a man make the transition from prison to a productive life on the outside if his children eventually take his place in prison. Although we have always tried to help the children and their mothers, we jumped in with both feet in 2010 when we launched our comprehensive full-time ministry to reach this underserved population, the families. We call it our Family and Children's Outreach Ministry, whose primary focus is to love, serve, and equip the families of men who are incarcerated—especially the children.

Jesus loves the little children, and so do we!

Led by MOV staff Tevin Peterson, Donna Mayo, Jennifer Wenberg, and Marlo Wilt, this exciting program has become hugely successful, thanks to the passion and commitment of the staff and many dedicated volunteers who give so freely of their time. Just look at all the things they do with the children and families of incarcerated men:

- One-on-one mentoring of children and mothers (our staff trains and supports these mentors).
- One-on-one tutoring to help kids stay ahead in school, and in the case of those out of school, we provide assistance to help them obtain a G.E.D.
- Large-scale events for the children such as lock-ins at local churches and fishing days--as in hooks and poles and worms at a nearby pond. Always these events are used to introduce the

kids to core values and beliefs through age-appropriate Bible lessons.

- Support groups for mothers led by volunteers who, based on their own experiences as successful parents, help moms cope with the challenges they face as single parents.
- M.O.V.E.—Men of Valor Entrepreneurs. This is an exciting after-school program for teens, designed to develop leadership, confidence, integrity, creativity, and a successful attitude through learning to run a micro-business.
- GLOW girls- God Leads Our Way. This group of girls in the nine-to-twelve age bracket meet once a week with Christian women who model for them how to become young ladies for God. Fellowship, fun, and food are center stage.
- Kid's night out/Mom's free night. Sometimes all a single mom needs is to have some time on her own to attend a church service, a class, or just put her feet up and relax. Our staff regularly take the kids out for a fun night so Mom can get a break from the day-to-day stress of managing her family.
- Church activities. We enjoy great partnerships with several local churches that willingly host these children for special concerts, worship gatherings, and other fun events. The more these young people are exposed to the Gospel

and learning biblical values, the greater chance they have to succeed in life.

- Sports. Getting kids involved in sports helps keep them out of trouble. It also teaches them teamwork, fair play, and discipline. We partner with some of the best sports camps and clinics available to give our youngsters quality instruction in the sports they are interested in. We also formed a partnership with the Ultimate Goal Soccer League for our six to eight-year old boys and girls.

- Fitness and nutritional training classes. We partner with the Donelson/ Hermitage YMCA to teach our moms and their kids the importance of exercise and a healthier diet. One of the many downsides of poverty is poor nutrition—often leading to obesity and other debilitating health conditions.

- Y-Literacy. This is a tutoring program for kids ages six through eighteen who have reading difficulties, provided through the Harding Place YMCA.

- B.E.S.T. Rewards System. An incentive program that enables youngsters to earn tangible rewards by doing community service, building character by teaching them to give back. Some of the rewards they can earn include tickets to Nashville Predators hockey games and

Nashville Sounds baseball games, as well as visits to the Tennessee Performing Arts Center to experience first class plays and musicals.

- Summer camp. All kids—especially city kids—need to experience summer camp, so through our partnership with the YMCA we provide our boys and girls with that opportunity at the Y's Camp Widjiwagan, and Barefoot Republic Camp through First Presbyterian Church, where they learn a variety of skills and grow in self-esteem, while having fun doing it.

- Christmas and birthday gifts for every child. Through the generosity of our volunteers and partnering churches, we make sure every child gets at least one present at Christmas and on his or her birthday. Without our help, there are children who wouldn't receive a single gift on those occasions.

- Transitional apartments for families. These are the apartments previously mentioned, supplied by Jimmy Webb, Bill Freeman, and Kirby Davis.

How do we do all this? As Tevin Peterson, the director of our children's ministry, puts it, "We believe God has a different destiny for children who have parents incarcerated. The number one indicator of a child's chances of ending up in prison is having a parent in prison. These kids were created for a purpose, and what we strive to do is bring the love of Jesus Christ into their lives at a young age to begin filling their minds with truth." That's where everything starts.

None of this would happen without the many people around the city who volunteer their time. Often they reach into their own pockets to provide a little something extra for a child or a mother. Still, any time I have had the pleasure of talking with our volunteers, they always tell me the same thing: "This does more for me than it does for them." They have experienced the joy of seeing a boy catch his very first fish, or the smile of a girl who scored her first goal, because someone volunteered to take him or her fishing or to soccer practices and games. Our volunteers are saints, as far as I'm concerned. They are living out the words of Jesus, who said, "Whatever you did for the least of these brothers of mine, you did for me." (Matthew 25:40, NIV)

These kids don't know what it's like to have a stable, normal life. Something as simple as going to a church concert or listening to someone tell a Bible story is foreign to them. If you grew up in a safe home and went to church as a child, you might think these things are commonplace, but to the children we work with, they are huge. I remember what it was like without any positive influences in my own young life, without a dad to teach me about baseball or take me camping. I vividly recall the sting of those words, "We don't want your kind around here." I did what any kid would do—I made my own "fun," and it got me into a lot of trouble.

That's the norm for these kids, which is why we are passionate about giving them hope by introducing them to the life-changing love of Jesus. The children and their moms greatly appreciate what we do for them. They have affection for their mentors and other volunteers. If smiles were money, our volunteers would be millionaires!

To give you an up close and personal look at how our family and children's ministry works, Tevin shares this story of a child who might have been lost to crime if it hadn't been for our investment in him:

DJ was eight years old when we first started working with him. His father was incarcerated, went through the Men of Valor program, and got out and was doing well when he was shot and killed. We made a commitment to his widow that we would be there for her and her kids. DJ was the oldest of four children, and he was filled with rage—furious at the world, angry at God, mad at everyone. He was clearly on a bad track and headed for trouble. We began working with him and connected him with a mentor. Today DJ is an example and leader to others. His grades went from below average to making the Dean's List. He's on the basketball team at his school. He's memorizing Bible verses. He's still only thirteen years old and has a long way to go, but he's turned the corner. He has a community of people who love him, and he knows that. Most important, he's got the Word of God in his mind to help him fight the assaults of the enemy.

Something tells me DJ is going to make it.

Although our primary focus of this aspect of MOV is children and their mothers, there's another benefit received from it: peace of mind for the incarcerated father. Few things are as discouraging to a man in prison as knowing his children are going through life without him. It eats away at him, often contributing to guilt and depression and an overall loss of hope and purpose. But when he knows Men of Valor is investing in his kids' lives, he is grateful and therefore motivated to keep doing the things he needs to do to one day become reunited with his family. While fathers in prison miss doing things with their kids, they take comfort in knowing a godly man or woman has stepped up to make sure their kids are being cared for. As one of our Jericho Project men wrote me, "You can only begin to imagine how much I truly appreciate what you did for my family at Christmas. I pray God will bless you back ten times for the blessing you have been to my children."

13

Does It Work?

When I started Men of Valor, my goal was simple: to disciple men and help those who get out of prison stay out of prison. If we could introduce them to the life-changing Gospel, then mentor them once they got out, they at least would have a chance of becoming successful, productive citizens. I knew the odds were against us because approximately seventy-percent of men who are released from prison return. It's called recidivism, and it's why our prisons have become profitable industries. In addition to new criminals entering the system, it is guaranteed that the majority of men released will be right back behind bars sooner or later. In Tennessee alone, the prison population has increased substantially since I was there. If these men have children on the outside, the majority of *them* are going to follow their fathers' footsteps.

"Rehabilitation" doesn't work. Rehabilitation implies getting a man back to where he was. For most of these men, that means getting them back to being poorly educated, without much direction, and suffering from the devastating effects of poverty. Instead of rehabilitation, we focus on *regeneration*—enabling these men to become something they had never been before. I could quote numbers to demonstrate our success, but the best way to illustrate what happens when we focus on regeneration is to quote directly from our men:

Anthony Charles

I grew up in a dysfunctional family that had no spiritual values. I didn't know there was a God; knew nothing about Jesus. My mom was the authority figure in our home. She had me when she was eighteen years old, and it seemed like she wanted a perfect child. To get that, she beat me perfect. As far back as I can remember she beat me multiple times a day with belts or extension cords. I wasn't allowed to be involved in activities outside the home. Instead she kept me inside and made me read books, including encyclopedias. I think she was trying to protect me from the bad things in the outside world, but she overdid it. There were times, however, when she could be very loving and did her best to make sure I got everything I needed.

The beatings went on until I was a junior in high school, when I finally decided I'd had enough and ran away. She tracked me down and I retaliated by secretly joining the military. Once I got into the military I discovered a whole new world of freedom I had never known before. I started drinking and soon became an alcoholic, although I didn't know it at the time. I was just doing what everyone else was doing. It seemed like they encouraged you to drink, though I'm not blaming anyone for my alcoholism.

Despite my drinking, I did well in the military, probably because my mother had groomed me for it; in fact, the military's discipline was easy compared to my mom's. I advanced through the ranks, making E-5 in four years, which was almost unheard of. But then I got busted with a DUI and the military gave me a choice: take a demotion and stay, or take severance pay and leave. I decided to leave, and that was the beginning of a long and downward spiral.

I moved back in with my mom in Chicago but not only kept right on drinking heavily but also started doing drugs. I stole some money from a girl, then decided to return to Nashville where I knew a friend who would let me live with him. The plan was to have one last big fling, then go back to Chicago and clean up my act. Somehow I never followed up on that plan. Instead, I sank deeper and deeper into drugs. Over the next ten years I was in and out of jail on various drug-related charges.

During my first jail term, someone told me about Jesus. For the first time in my life I learned that he died on the cross for my sins. I accepted him as my Savior but not as my Lord, so when I got out of jail I kept living only for myself. I considered myself saved, but that didn't change the way I lived. It wasn't long before I was back in jail. Each time I served my sentence and got out, I sought out my old friends and returned to using drugs, until I got seriously busted. This time I was sent to prison, which was probably the best thing that ever happened to me. That's where I learned about Men of Valor.

I was fortunate to be accepted into The Jericho Project (one of MOV's programs), which is an intense curriculum designed to turn me into the man God intended me to be. I approached it just as I did the military—highly disciplined. I studied the Bible carefully and learned all about God and his love for me. But for me this was simply an accomplishment, an achievement. Despite all the hard work, when I got out I suffered a couple of setbacks. Yet still those guys from Men of Valor poured themselves into me. They never gave up on me.

One day it was like I heard God actually speaking to me. He said, "You experienced all my blessings. You know who I am. But you don't know Jesus." That changed everything for me. I realized it wasn't just about knowing what the Bible said but about having a personal relationship with Jesus Christ. Going through The Jericho Project gave me the foundation of truth that I needed, but it wasn't until I let Jesus become Lord of my life that I began to turn my life around. I knew I couldn't have a relationship with him and still do drugs, so I turned away from drugs and haven't gone back. I went through the Couchville after-care program, which had a big impact on me as well.

Men of Valor showed me it wasn't enough to just change my ways, because I could always change back. They taught me that I had to literally become a new person. Romans 12:2 says that we need to be "transformed by the renewing of the mind." Men of Valor helped me do that. They stay with you and walk the difficult journey with you. Always before I had tried to change on my own, but that was futile. I thought I could just work my way to a better life, but without surrendering your life completely to Jesus Christ, you just can't do it.

Today, I'm on staff at Men of Valor as an Aftercare Coordinator/Crew Team Leader. All the bad things that happened in my life, God turned around for good, and now I have the opportunity to influence the same type of guy I used to be. Just the other day I met with a man who I had mentored at Couchville while he served for six months on my work crew. Now he's out on his own and living independently as a productive citizen. He now even volunteers with Men of Valor two days a week. It is such a powerful thing to remember where he used to be and see where he is today. It almost gives me more pleasure to see this happen in other guys' lives than in my own.

It's all God, man.

AC, as we call him, is one of five guys who were once incarcerated, went through our program, and are now on staff at MOV. They're all doing a great job and have enormous credibility with the men they work with. They serve as great role models, proving to our men that they can make it on the outside, too, if they stick with the program.

And now, Marcus Martin tells his story:

Marcus Martin

I grew up in a stable family. My parents were together and provided for us well. But after a house fire destroyed a record collection, I moved out and struggled with depression. The reason my record collection was so important to me was that my dad had helped me build a recording studio and I had hopes of going into the music business. I still wanted to do that, so I started stealing to get enough money to rebuild. I had never had a drop to drink, but I went into a liquor store and asked the clerk what would really get the job done. He pointed to the shelf and said, "Take your pick." My eyes landed on a bottle of Tanqueray gin and from that day forward I started drinking it straight. To earn a little money I began selling weed and using it, too. I got caught and was sent to prison. It wasn't long before a fellow inmate invited me to a Bible study, but I told him I didn't want anything to do with God. About a year later I went to one of the Bible studies because I was bored and needed the excuse to get out of my cell. That's where I first learned about Jesus, but I didn't really understand the whole thing about being born again. Later, the leader of that Bible study asked me if I wanted to accept Jesus as my Savior and I said I would. He took me into a little empty cell and I basically followed the teaching of Romans 10: 9-10: "If you confess with your mouth that Jesus is Lord and believe in your heart that God raised him from the dead, you will be saved."

Then he told me about Men of Valor, and I started attending a class led by Carl Carlson. I can still hear his deep voice as he spoke about integrity and pounded the table for emphasis. I wanted to have what he had, so over the rest of my time in prison I attended the Bible studies and other programs of Men of Valor, even leading some of the classes myself. When I was released, Men of Valor set me up with a job at a cabinet-making company, which was a great blessing. One of the hardest things for a man with a record is finding a job. Even though I was officially out on my own, I continued attending Men of Valor Bible studies. After about a year and a half, Carl offered me a job, and now I'm full-time with MOV, working at CCA. None of this would have happened without God and the great teachers and mentors of Men of Valor.

Marcus goes to prison every day now—five days a week. He even has an office there. He has become a beacon of hope for men just like himself who have made mistakes. They too, can turn the corner to follow Jesus. Sometimes, though, transformation doesn't happen quite so quickly, as you'll see in the next story:

Frank Turner

Like many young men in the city, I began drinking and drugging in my teenage years, and when you do drugs it isn't long before you start stealing to support your habit. You never think you're going to get caught, but you always do. So over a period of about twenty years I was in and out of jail and prison seven times.

Each time when I got sent back to jail, I would cry out to God. I accepted Jesus into my life and spent time studying the Scriptures. When I got out, however, I'd stay clean for a few weeks then go right back to using again. It was during my last prison sentence that I learned about The Jericho Project offered by Men of Valor. I had tried other programs offered by the state to help me get off drugs and stay out of trouble, but they never worked. The Jericho Project was different. They poured themselves into me, feeding me spiritually. They taught me that the Greek word for Holy Spirit is "comforter," which means helper. I had always expected Jesus to just heal me instantly like he did for the woman with the issue of blood and other people who had physical illnesses. But through The Jericho Project I learned that addiction is a habit of the flesh—there's no miracle cure for it. I learned to face my addiction and let the Holy Spirit help me stand against the temptation to use. It's been eight years since I got out, and I've been clean the whole time.

The Jericho Project helped me discover gifts that I never knew I had, like speaking to groups of men, writing—I've written two books—and connecting Scripture with everyday experiences men face.

One year after I got out of prison, Carl hired me, and I've been with MOV ever since. My current role is managing our Couchville property, which I do in the evenings. But The

Jericho Project also taught me job skills which have helped me run my own business during the day.

Men of Valor is making whole men out of broken men by the power of God to the glory of God. That's what they did for me, and now I'm trying to give back to other men who need someone to walk beside them and show them the way.

One of the common denominators for the men we work with is poverty. When you don't have much and see people who seem to have everything, it does something to your value system, as you'll learn from the next man sharing his story:

Chad Daniels

With my dad out of the picture and my mom suffering from mental illness, I was raised by my grandmother, who not only raised her own three daughters, but their children as well. She did it on the wages of a grocery store clerk. I'd already gotten involved with drugs and seen the kind of money that was exchanged, so I started robbing drug dealers to help my grandmother pay the bills. I justified it by thinking I was robbing from the greedy to give to the poor. I knew it was dangerous, but I had already considered committing suicide because we lived such a miserable life, so I thought, "What difference will it make if I get killed by one of the dealers?"

As it turned out, I was caught and received a stiff prison sentence. I didn't know it at the time, but God was working on me. He is sovereign, and he orders our steps. After a few years, I heard about a man who came into the prison once a week and conducted Bible studies. His name was Carl Carlson. I started going to his Bible studies, and they completely changed my life. I not only committed myself to the Lord Jesus Christ, but I learned what it means to be a godly man. Carl was a man just like me, but he had turned his life over to Jesus and now was ministering to me and others like me—men like himself. Today I am working for Men of Valor aiming to do for others what Carl did for me. Every day I drive the same streets where I used to rob drug dealers, and I realize that if it wasn't for the Lord Jesus Christ, I'd either still be in prison or I'd be dead.

Chad married his high school sweetheart, Sherry, and recently they welcomed their first child, a daughter. People sometimes ask me if I ever worry about hiring men from our program. I'd hire them all if I had enough money! I don't need a background check to tell me they've had some problems, but I know how hard they had to work to get through our program. After successfully completing The Jericho Project and our after-care program, these guys have earned my trust and respect. They have tremendous credibility with the people they work for

One last story for you. I began working with a young lady named Jennifer Wenberg because she was a long-time friend of one of my sons. Jennifer's parents both struggled with drugs and alcohol all her life. Her mom's drug use landed her in jail a few times, and because her parents were divorced and neither was able to give her the care she needed, Jennifer was raised mostly by her grandmother. Today, she works in our family and children's ministry program, pouring her life into the hearts and souls of young girls.

Jennifer Wenberg

If it wasn't for my grandma teaching me about Jesus, I don't think I would have made it. Because I know what it's like to be in an unstable family with drugs and alcohol and jail, I have a burden for kids who are growing up in those situations. It's never easy because these kids have seen so much. Sometimes they rebel against you, but I understand why and just keep telling them, "I know it's hard. I've been there too. But God loves you and has a purpose for you, so don't give up." These kids are used to adults letting them down, so when a mentor shows up when they say they will, it's huge. Sometimes they just need to know they can trust someone. I love what I do. No, it's not easy, but I love it!

While we've had enormous success, not every man we work with stays clean and sober. Some end up back in prison. Every year I learn about one of the kids in our family and children's program who has gotten into serious trouble. The truth is, there are times when the frustrations outnumber the rewards.

But I no longer get too frustrated over our so-called failures. In fact, I no longer think of them as failures. We've given our men, their wives, and the children the Gospel. We've planted a seed in their hearts. We've shown them the love that only Jesus offers. The rest is up to the Holy Spirit and that particular individual. We have no idea what may be down the road for anyone in a year from now, five years from now, or ten years. We simply trust that God is in control and for whatever reason we were unable to see the transformation take place.

We do the best we can, all by the light God has given us. The rest is up to him and the individual. When you stop to think about it, the same applies to all of us. You might be a twenty-six year old just getting out of prison, or a sixty-two year old businessman thinking of retirement. What are you going to do with the days and years God gives you, starting right now?

14

Not My Legacy, But God's

Once again, I did not set out to write this book. Over the years different men would say to me, Carl, you need to write a book, and my answer was always the same: No thanks! As much as God has removed my guilt through his Son's sacrifice, it's not easy going back and recounting some of the things I've experienced and done. Even with Men of Valor's success, which I'm delighted with, I do not want to shine a spotlight on myself in any way.

Jeff Dobyns, one of MOV's board members, a good friend and loyal supporter, softened my resolve one day. He explained that one reason I should share my story in book form is to leave a legacy for my sons. Jeff knows how much I love my sons and want God's absolute best for them. The more I thought about what he said, the more I began thinking that the legacy I wanted to leave for my boys is not about me, but about God.

The real story here is not about my messed up past or even the work Men of Valor is doing. It is that with God, anything is possible. He has a plan and a purpose for every one of us if we turn our lives over to him. (Jeremiah 29:11) My story is the oldest and most repeated one known to man: I once was lost but now am found. The greatest miracle God can perform is to change a person's heart. It doesn't mean you become a perfect person. It means you have God on your side, and with him, all things are possible.

By man's way of looking at things, I shouldn't even be alive, let alone helping change the lives of incarcerated men and their families. I could easily have lost my life in that first police chase where I crashed into a ditch with my little brother. It could have been a tree or another car instead of a ditch. I could have been one of the 11,616 soldiers killed during the year I served in Vietnam. From then until I finally came to my senses, I dodged many bullets. Being a bouncer at a New Jersey nightclub isn't the safest profession. Getting shot by police or other criminals is one of the occupational hazards of robbing jewelry stores. I knew many guys who overdosed or drank themselves to death, but that didn't stop me from drugging and drinking. And prison? Every time you left your cell, you watched your back in case someone wanted to settle a score with a shiv to your gut.

If God can take an orphan boy bent on a life of destruction and make something of him, think of what he can do for you! That's all the "legacy" I wish to leave. If you've invited Jesus into your life, you can't just stay where you are. The Bible says, "to whom much is given, much is required." (Luke 12:48) We've been given the greatest gift possible—eternal life and the peace that comes from being forgiven. This means we need to give back; not because we have to, but because it's such a privilege to serve in the name of Jesus. When you take a look at the world we live in, there are plenty of opportunities for giving back. George Bernard Shaw once wrote:

> *This is the true joy in life, the being used for a purpose recognized by yourself as a mighty one; the being a force of nature instead of a feverish selfish clod of ailments and grievances complaining that the world will not devote itself to making you happy. I am of the opinion that my life belongs to the whole community and as long as I live it is my privilege to do for it whatever I can. I want to be thoroughly used up when I die, for the harder I work, the more I live. I rejoice in life for its own sake. Life is no 'brief candle' to me. It is sort of a splendid torch which I have a hold of for the moment,*

> *and I want to make it burn as brightly as*
> *possible before handing it over to future*
> *generations.*

Wouldn't it be something if everyone who is a Christian decided to get serious about giving back? Let us never be among those who complain and criticize things we don't like. The best way to make something better is to jump in and get to work. Instead of complaining about our nation's abortion laws, volunteer at a crisis pregnancy center to walk alongside a young woman trying to decide what to do about her unplanned pregnancy. Consider volunteering at The Hope Clinic, for instance.

Think of our nation's schools. It's clear we have an education crisis, and there are plenty of people and policies to blame. But what would happen if our schools were flooded with an army of volunteers to mentor at-risk kids? I've seen what can happen when a struggling child receives regular special attention from a caring adult. Teachers love it when our Men of Valor volunteers mentor their more challenging students. It won't solve all our problems with education, but complaining and criticizing solves none of them.

You don't have to be an orphan or a former prisoner to live the way Jesus invites you to live. According to him, Christians are a light in the darkness and the salt of the earth. You can let your light shine, not for your own glory but so that others "may see your good deeds and praise your Father in heaven." (Matthew 5:15, NIV) Whenever someone asks our mentors why they volunteer their time to work with men in prison or their families, they explain how their Christian faith motivates everything they do. Some people think Christianity is only about going to church and following a set of rules, but it's about loving people the way Jesus loved us. This is why I am so proud of our staff and the hundreds of volunteers who quietly go about their mission of loving people in the name of Jesus.

Author Bob Buford wrote in his book, *Half Time,* that when we get to heaven, God is going to ask us two questions: "What did you do about Jesus?" and "What did you do with all I gave you?" Perhaps you've already answered the Jesus question and accepted him as your Savior. If not, may you do that today. He didn't just save my soul, he saved my life. The Bible is clear about salvation: "Believe in the Lord Jesus Christ and you will be saved." (Acts 16:31, NIV)

If you live in the Nashville area, we can find a place for you to help turn broken men into whole men for God or help their families live better lives. You could join our team and support us with your skills and talents, or give financially.

Wherever you live, there are people near you who are hurting and in need of the same love that lifted you and me from our sin and despair. Take that first step in becoming the hands and feet of Jesus in your community.

Please pray for the Men of Valor ministry.

If you are interested in learning more about Men of Valor, our web site address is www.men-of-valor.org

May God richly bless you and your family.

15

The Final Chapter

by Karen Carlson

It was the first week of October 2014, and Carl and I were celebrating our 34th anniversary in the beautiful wilds of Wyoming—a gift from our friends Jack and Lisle Hooper. While there, we received word from our daughter-in-law, Janna, that this book had been finished. We were delighted! It had been a long road. My tenderhearted husband took my hand and said to me, as he so often did, "Honey, let's pray."

He thanked God for the book's completion, then prayed a blessing over it. He asked that only God, and not himself, be glorified in its pages. He prayed that readers' hearts might be touched and their lives changed by the presence of the Holy Spirit. He added a fervent request for the Lord to continue to guide and protect our children, our church, and our country. Last, he beseeched God to keep his hand on the Men of Valor staff and volunteers, families and inmates, benefactors and prayer partners. When he was finished praying, he looked at me and said, "If my story will help others, I'm glad it's being told."

Exactly one week later, my beloved went home. He died in his sleep, with no struggle and no suffering. His earthly journey had come to an end, and the great warrior's heart beat its last. He was instantly present with the Lord.

Well done, good and faithful servant.

Carl's childhood and youth were filled with pain and struggle, some of which has been described in these pages. God restored the years that had been lost, but this isn't to say the rest of his life would be easy. It never was. Even after being saved, he knew many hardships. The good news is, he was able to take those hardships, turn them over to Jesus, and move forward, using their life-lessons to help others. He was working to that end until the very last night of his life. God's servant died just as he had lived… and he went out with his boots on.

He had great joy, too. Our marriage—he and I sharing the life God designed for us—kept us grounded and secure. Our four sons were his strength, pride, and comfort. He loved them with his whole heart. His work—the calling upon his life—was a magnificent gift from God. His faith enabled him to persevere with courage, while looking to Jesus for wisdom and direction. His heart was always, always with others:

family, friends, and the downtrodden. He was not perfect and would not want me to turn him into a saint now that he's gone. But he was a man transformed and, shortcomings and all, he labored for the Kingdom. Now, he lives with the King!

No eye has seen, no ear has heard, no mind can conceive what God has prepared for those who love him. (I Corinthians 2:9) I can almost hear Carl calling to me: "Babe! If you could only see what I'm seeing and know what I know! All those sufferings down there— no matter how terrible—aren't worth comparing to the glory that is revealed here! (Romans 8:18) I can hardly wait to show you around. Stay strong, remain faithful, look up. And tell our boys to do the same. Tell everyone!"

One day, we who are Christ's followers, will live on the New Earth, where, thank our Holy God, there will be no prisons. No bars. No ridicule or despair or shame. No darkness and no fear. Until then, I hope you will serve the Lord in whatever way he calls you. For he definitely has plans for you. (see Jeremiah 29:11-13) No matter who you are or where you have been, you can know Jesus in the same way Carl did. Just seek his will with all your heart, and you will find it.

As for me and my house, we will serve the Lord. ~ Joshua 24:15